The Age of Accountability

The Age of Accountability

Jerry Boritzki

Copyright © 2024 Jerry Boritzki
All rights reserved
ISBN 9798989480401

Why this book?

Ask yourself. Ask your pastor. Contact any Bible college or seminary and ask them to explain to you two things:

1. What is the age of accountability?
2. At what age does one become eternally accountable for their sins?

Chances are you, your pastor and college/seminary will have a vague understanding of what the definition might be (likely based on only one verse concerning David's infant son) but no idea whatsoever when one's accountability begins. This lack of knowledge is a spiritual travesty. This doctrine, when fully understood and embraced, will magnify the attributes of God in ways you could never have imagined.

Contents

Preface..ix

Introduction...xi

Chapter 1 – What You Likely Know and Don't Know Concerning the
    Age of Accountability.. 1
    Definition of the Age of Accountability 5

Chapter 2 – There Must Be a Biblical Answer......................................11

Chapter 3 – Different Views 15

Chapter 4 – Considering the Law of First Mention 19

Chapter 5 – Biblical Age for Military Service......................................27

Chapter 6 – Biblical View of Levitical Service 33

Chapter 7 – The Exodus...39

Chapter 8 – Scripture and Accountability 47

Chapter 9 – The Science 53

Chapter 10 – When Sin Is Not Imputed 59

Chapter 11 – From Twenty Years Old and Upward 65

Chapter 12 – A Later Age Fits with the Attributes of God..................67

Chapter 13 – How Does This Affect My Life and My Ministry?..............71

Appendix I 75

Appendix II...77

Appendix III 79

About the Author 81

Preface

Today, if someone writes a book on Bible-related subjects, they may start out with an apology. An apology is given by the author because the book they are writing has already been written. In fact, there might be dozens or even hundreds of books written on that subject. If the title of a new book is Romans or The Life of Paul we have to ask ourselves just how much new information can be written on these subjects. So, the majority of these books are primarily a review and rewording of hundreds of authors before them. To be fair, most authors have found a nugget of fresh information to add to a subject.

This book has no predecessor; no book has been written on the age of accountability that I have been able to locate. No clever title needed to be created as no book on this subject has ever been written. The web site was easily purchased with the same name because there are no websites dealing with this all-important doctrine.

Not only is there no book on this subject but I would like to challenge you to think about a few things for a moment. First, ask yourself what is the age of accountability? What do I know about the age of accountability? Definition? When does one become eternally accountable to God for their sins? Ask a few of your friends the same questions. Find out what other people know about this subject. When they give you their thoughts, ask them if they have any biblical reason for their opinions. Then, if you attend church somewhere, ask your pastor those same questions. If you accept this challenge, you will quickly learn why I had to write this book and why you need to read this book.

The subject of the age of accountability is a missing piece of information in Christianity today. It seems no one knows anything about it. I have found most people have a fairly good definition of the term but their knowledge ends there. What age that definition is activated seems to be relegated to one of the great mysteries of the Bible. Why is this subject left unexplored when in fact, it is one of the great truths of Scripture that God wants us to understand?

A clear Biblical understanding of the age of accountability offers clarity to so many other Bible truths: a shining fresh light on the very attributes of God, a new meaning to what it means to be a parent, a pastor, a Sunday School teacher or Children's Church worker. We can genuinely rest in God's Word and allow God to work in our young people's lives.

Introduction

The average pastor, church member, parent or teacher has no understanding of when a person becomes eternally accountable to God for their sins. And yet, to a born-again believer, this is the most important subject in our life concerning our children and those we are ministering to. Because of this lack of knowledge there is an unrest in their hearts, a panic of urgency that should not be there. Here we are, we know that *"...all have sinned and come short of the glory of God"* **Romans 3:23**. We know that *"...the wages of sin is death, but the gift of God is eternal life through Jesus Christ our Lord"* **Romans 6:23**. We have this great truth committed to memory, but we don't know when God will hold those around us accountable for the wages of their sin. When, exactly, is our son or daughter, our congregation or student responsible, eternally, for his or her sins? In our thinking, these wages, this eternal judgement for their sins, hangs over our children like the sword of Damocles. Where do we learn in Scripture that God will behave like (and I refer to Cicero concerning the sword of Damocles) "the tyrannical king" who hung a sword over a courtier because he made light of the great responsibilities of a king?

The goal of this book is to shine light on a great truth, a doctrine clearly understood and followed throughout Scripture yet completely overlooked in today's theology. This Bible truth is perhaps the answer to why so many of our young people are leaving the church, why our young people are rejecting the wonderful truths they were taught in good Christian homes. If we could better understand the grace and longsuffering of our God towards our youth, we could remove the pressure that parents and church leaders feel concerning the urgency of seeing young people saved at such young ages and let them enjoy the learning of God's plan for each one of them.

It is said that a parent should never have to bury their child. With street crimes, drunk drivers, drug overdoses and even a heartbreaking increase in teenage suicides, the responsibility of every Christian is to be ready to give an answer to every parent. The one thing that complicates the loss of every young person is not knowing where that child will spend eternity. At a family's time of greatest need, if you do not understand the age of accountability, you can offer no real comfort. What hope can you offer if you have no knowledge on this subject? We tell our family and friends that our faith is not a "hope so, but a know so" faith. But do you know what the Bible teaches on the subject of a young person and the age of accountability?

Chapter 1

What You Likely Know and Don't Know Concerning the Age of Accountability

Very likely the story of David and his son is the sum total of your knowledge concerning the age of accountability. Even with this limited knowledge you understand God will not send an aborted child to Hell nor will He send an infant to Hell. But where do you go from this one verse? That is the important truth this book explores.

Allow me to take you, with your current Bible knowledge concerning the age of accountability, into a local funeral home. A young mother has lost her newborn just hours or perhaps days after birth. This mother comes to you with tears flowing down her flushed and weary cheeks and asks you where her baby is today. With the confidence that we can have only through the power of God's Word we are able to comfort this distraught parent with the same words that David used to explain why he ended his fast and was already getting back to his daily responsibilities following his son's illness and subsequent premature death. David, understanding God's grace, responds to those who do not understand the doctrine of "the age of accountability" in **2 Samuel 12:23a,** *"But now he is dead, wherefore should I fast? can I bring him back again…?"* David is at total peace with the knowledge that though his son has died he, David, will one day be eternally reunited with his son in Heaven. One day David will die and he says in the same verse **2 Samuel 12:23**, *"...I shall go to him".*

This one verse seems to be all the average Christian and even the majority of pastors know on the age of accountability. The subject is ignored in pulpits and Bible colleges all around the world. I speak from experience. This one verse is the only training I had concerning this all-important subject though I have both a bachelors as well as a masters degree in religious education. For some unknown reason this subject is skirted, avoided and ultimately ignored and forgotten. It seems unimportant until a friend or church member comes to you asking the most important question they have ever asked anyone in their life. "Where is my little boy?" "Where is my little girl right now?"

But now he is dead, wherefore should I fast? can I bring him back again? I shall go to him, but he shall not return to me.

– 2 Samuel 12:23

We immediately understand the importance of this doctrine by simply reading the next verse. With simple confidence David is able to take his understanding of God and, with authority, is able to comfort his wife. With Holy Spirit inspiration we learn in **2 Samuel 12:24**, *"...David comforted...his wife...".* Is it not our desire to be able to comfort those around us with the truth of God's Word on any subject? Of course it is. **1 Thessalonians 4:18**, *"Wherefore comfort one another with these words."* **1 Thessalonians 5:11**, *"Wherefore comfort yourselves together, and edify one another, even as also ye do."* Do you feel prepared to offer comfort based on what you currently know on the subject of the age of accountability?

If you have that genuine desire to comfort the brethren, let us go back to the funeral home. This young mother, though still brokenhearted realizes that her beautiful baby is in the loving arms of our Savior and you can watch as this comforted mother shows the signs of hope that can come only from God's inspired and eternal Word.

You are thrilled to have been able to be God's instrument in such a difficult and sensitive situation. Now...let's return to the funeral home, with a changing scenario. You walk in, but this time the child lying there is one year old. Likely you will have nearly the same confidence in your understanding of Scripture to tell this grieving mother the same comforting truth. You might even go into a short explanation of what we call the "age of accountability". The mother gladly receives this good counsel and with tears still in her eyes you see in her the same hope that David and his wife once enjoyed at such a difficult time. The parents go home knowing they will once again see their beloved child. Once again, you are able to return home excited to be a part of God's plan of bringing real peace to the world.

But...what if the scenario goes on and the child lying there was:

– 3 years old?
– 4 years old?
– 5 years old?
– 6 years old?
– 7 years old?
– 8, 9, 10 years old?
– 12 years old?
– 14 years old?
– 18 years old?

Do you see the problem? Though you have a working knowledge of the definition of the age of accountability, at what age does that child biblically become accountable for their sins? What age do you "think" he or she becomes accountable? Most importantly what does God specifically say concerning the "age of accountability"? At what age could you no longer bring the comfort so desperately needed because you do not have a Bible knowledge on this subject? The purpose of this book is to answer this all-important question. You do not want to be standing in front of a broken-hearted parent or grandparent with that empty and powerless clichéd phrase, "Only God can really know that". Particularly if that is not a true biblical statement. If that is all you can leave the family with when you leave that funeral home, you will feel as empty as that grieving family.

In 1974 as a young sailor stationed thousands of miles from home I was told, by an excited coworker, that I could KNOW that Heaven would one day be my eternal home. The very thought that anyone could "know" anything so wonderful was overwhelming to me. This coworker shared **1 John 5:13,** *"These things* *have I written unto you that believe on the name of the Son of God; that ye may know that ye have eternal life, and that ye may believe on the name of the Son of God."* That simple truth made all the difference to me. This is the great difference between the denominational church I grew up in, where you could never "know" for sure about Heaven, and the Bible-believing church I one morning attended where I stepped out into the aisle at the invitation and immediately knew Heaven was my home. The Bible gives us assurance. It gives us knowledge and hope. As we so often hear, it is not a "hope so" but a "KNOW SO" faith. This is God's desire for every one of us, regardless of age.

Now, are we to accept that we can "know" those from birth to perhaps two or four years of age have eternal life, but that there is some gap of time where we simply can't "know" if they do or do not have eternal life? Do we believe that God has some period of time, a "Twilight Zone" period when no one really knows if a young person is lost or saved? Then, perhaps years later, when they have made the decision to accept Christ, once again we, with great confidence now "know" again?

It seems most Christians and certainly the vast majority of pastors, know there is Bible doctrine referred to as the age of accountability. They can, to some degree give you a textbook definition of what the phrase means. What no one seems to be able to tell you is what are the parameters of that "age". Simply, at what age do we become accountable to God for our sins? That is the purpose of this book.

Let's visit that funeral home one last time. You tell the mother of a four-year-old that her child is in Heaven. She seems relieved but then asks you, "How do you know that?", "What exactly is the age of accountability"? You try to go into a deeper explanation, but she stops you. She wants to know the chronological age that one will become responsible (eternally accountable) for their sins. How do you know that her child, at that specific age, that specific day is, in fact, in Heaven? If you have to tell her that you don't really know the age...but you feel sure her son or daughter would fall into the period "covered", then you need to keep reading. When even you do not feel good about your answer and it is clear she is not being comforted by your words, it is time to understand God in this matter.

In the following pages it is my prayer and desire to give you the Scriptures, the tools, and the confidence to fill the gap of understanding concerning the age of innocence and the age of accountability so that you can walk into any situation and help all people of all ages.

Working Definition and Understanding Of "the Age of Accountability"

That moment in time, and following, when one becomes eternally responsible and "accountable" to God for both their sin nature as well as their individual sins. Conversely, God gives to every person a period, prior to being held accountable, in which one is not accountable to God, for either their sins, their sin nature or even their unbelief and rejection of God. This period we recognize as the age of "innocence" and is offered only because of God's unsearchable grace.

Paul clearly understood this time of "innocence" in his own life. He speaks of that period in his life when the Law did not pertain to him; a time when the Law existed but he was "alive" in spite of the Law and man's responsibility to the Law. Then, one day, it did come into his life. **Romans 7:9,** *"For I was alive without the Law once: but when the commandment came, sin revived, and I died."* This statement becomes more interesting when you think of how Paul had been trained in the Law and religion from birth. **Acts 22:3,** *"I am verily a man which am a Jew, born in Tarsus, a city in Cilicia, yet brought up in this city at the feet of Gamaliel, and taught according to the perfect manner of the Law of the fathers, and was zealous toward God, as ye all are this day."* Not only did the Law exist, but Paul was well trained in that Law. However, during some period of his life he was not accountable before God for the Law. We see there was a time prior to accepting Christ when Paul was still spiritually alive.

In **Romans 7:9,** Paul points out that he *"...was alive without the law once"* (past tense) then, at some point in his life he became guilty because the Law **"came"** to him. Without the Law sin is dead, but when the Law pertains to us, it convicts us. Think of it like driving on a country road at 50 miles an hour. You see a sign that reads "Bridge Out Ahead"; it is a warning of things to come. There is nothing wrong with the sign. Note, it is not the sign that is your enemy, nor is the bridge out because of the sign. The sign is simply warning you of what will, eventually, affect you. The bridge being out, will be a very big problem to you if you continue to drive 50 miles an hour. So long as the bridge is still miles ahead you are completely free of the problem. Though it is already out, it does not affect you at that moment. Perhaps along the way people are waving, yelling, begging you to go back. Clearly, they are signaling you to take the "right road". But so far as you can see, there is no problem. Normally the signs even tell you when it will affect you; two miles ahead, one mile ahead, 500 feet ahead. Eventually, that which had no affect on you is now the most important thing in your life. If you continue doing the exact same speed that you have been doing "safely" for the past 50 miles, the very thing that did not impact you at all one second ago is the very thing that will now take your life. This is exactly what Paul refers to in the verses leading up to his proclamation that there was a time in his life that he was free from the law **"once"**. Rom 7:7-8, *"What shall we say then? Is the law sin? God forbid. Nay, I had not known sin, but by the Law: for I had not known lust, except the law had said, Thou shalt not covet. But sin, taking occasion by the commandment, wrought in me all manner of concupiscence. For without the law sin was dead."*

Romans 7:9, *"For I was alive without the law once: but when the commandment came, sin revived, and I died."* Here we see Paul in his youth, is alive freely driving along at 50 mph and not responsible for this upcoming problem. Then, at some point in his life that period ended, and he became responsible to the Law and he then **"died".**

As Paul found, once we are responsible for our sins we have "died" and because we have **"died"** (spiritually) we are in desperate need of being **"born again"** John 3:3,7. This is a beautiful picture of what Christ did for us. He died that we might live. Dead in our sins, we can trust in the finished work of Jesus Christ on Calvary and have life, abundant life, eternal life.

Through these truths we learn there is a period of time when the Law can warn us but not condemn us. This would be the age of innocence leading us one day to the age of accountability. It is important to note that we are given plenty of time to get off the road leading to the danger. The decision to change our course can be made at any point prior to reaching that bridge. Paul reached the bridge and **"died"**...then, at a later date...was born again.

Not only is it possible to be aware of the Law when we are not **"under"** the Law but we can take it a step further. It is possible during this same time to be responsible for the consequences of that law...and yet not to be guilty when breaking that law. We have an illustration of this truth available to us. Embassy workers throughout the world have what is called, "diplomatic immunity". All the laws are in effect around them, and they are expected to obey all the laws of the country they are living in, but, if they should break the law, they are **immune** from all punishment. We could say they are not accountable for the very laws they are directed to obey. Though expected and required to obey the laws, they cannot be punished for breaking any of those laws. During our time of **"innocence"** we are driving down the road with **"immunity"**. But there are signs (Scripture, parents, pastors, billboards) telling us that things are going to change: Bridge Out Ahead. The moment we arrive at the location of the bridge, we will be held accountable for the very laws we have been told to obey all of our lives. I have thought, perhaps, a better term than "age of innocence" might be "age of immunity" to help everyone understand this truth more accurately.

When we receive Christ as Savior, we are given life and are made free from the Law. When under the Law and accountable to that Law...we die. The Law condemns us. **Romans 8:2**, *"For the Law of the Spirit of life in Christ Jesus hath made me free from the law of sin and death."*

It is with particular interest that we should read of the rebellion of God's people in the wilderness wanderings. The Psalmist refers to this time period in **Psa 95:10**, *"Forty years long was I grieved with this generation, and said, It is a people that do err in their heart, and they have not known my ways"* Then there is a promise made to those with whom He is grieved. To all those who have not known His ways he makes a promise: **Psa 95:11**, *"Unto whom I sware in my wrath that they should not enter into my rest."*

In Chapter 5 of this book we will cast more light on the innocence of children and the "accountability" of all others. We will see why **"they"** (in Psa 95:11 above) should not enter into God's rest, but all the others will. Please keep reading. The understanding of the "age of accountability" will change your life forever, as it has mine.

In the New Testament, Jesus gives us a baseline we must meet if we are to ever see Heaven. That baseline, that standard, is that we must become (again) as a child. **Mark 10:14-15**, *"But when Jesus saw it, he was much displeased, and said unto them, Suffer the little children to come unto me, and forbid them not: for of such is the kingdom of God. Verily I say unto you, Whosoever shall not receive the kingdom of God as a little child, he shall not enter therein."*

This truth is so important that we see it taught in a little different light in another of the Gospels. **Matthew 18:3-4**, *"...Verily I say unto you, Except ye be converted, and become as little children, ye shall not enter into the kingdom of heaven.*

Whosoever therefore shall humble himself as this little child, the same is greatest in the kingdom of heaven". Isn't it interesting that this verse does not say we need to be like a little child and with childlike faith be converted? Rather, through this conversion we once again become as we once were. Free from the Law...and once again innocent (immune) in God's sight. In both the Old and the New Testaments, we find two separate groups of people: those not accountable for the Law and those who are accountable to the Law, the innocent (in God's sight) and the accountable, the saved and the unsaved, the righteous and the unrighteous. Let's see how age affects our accountability towards God's law and commands.

We now see that God views two groups of people, though completely different, in a similar way. Those who are innocent by reason of not having reached the age of accountability and those who are saved and called righteous. Ex 23:7, *"Keep thee far from a false matter; and the innocent and righteous slay thou not: for I will not justify the wicked."* We see, in fact, three groups now: innocent, righteous and wicked.

>**Innocent** – prior to the age of accountability.
>**Righteous** – those who have become accountable and are with God.
>**Wicked** – those who have become accountable and are without God.

In Psa 106, God gives us an insight as to how He views youth...innocent. **Psa 106:38,** *"And shed innocent blood, even the blood of their sons and of their daughters, whom they sacrificed unto the idols of Canaan: and the land was polluted with blood."* Innocent is not only describing infants but the "younger" generation as well.

It is eternally important that we understand the difference between being without sin, and not being accountable for that sin. Or, in the case of youth, being immune from the eternal penalty for sin. The Bible makes it abundantly clear that we are all sinners. **Rom 3:23,** *"For all have sinned, and come short of the glory of God;"*

We know this includes children both born and in their mothers' wombs. **Psa 51:5,** *"Behold, I was shapen in iniquity; and in sin did my mother conceive me."* We are all sinners in God's eyes. We all sin. Yet God calls young people "innocent". Interesting that in **Psa 106:38** above, God refers to "innocent blood". The definition of this word innocent, according to Strong's Hebrew definition is "blameless, clean, clear, free, guiltless and (importantly to this study) **exempted**".

Those not yet "accountable" for their sins are guiltless and are exempted by the only One who can exempt them, God.

Once we look at all the Scripture and all the examples in Scripture, it becomes very difficult to deny this time of innocence when God does not hold a young person eternally accountable for their sins.

Putting it all together, unless we are or become as little children...blameless, guiltless and exempted, we will never see or enter the kingdom of Heaven.

Chapter 2

There Must Be a Biblical Answer

I have to assume you are reading this book because you are seeking biblical truth concerning the age of innocence and accountability. Though some take the position that there is no such thing as the age of innocence, these are in such a minority and without any scriptural basis whatsoever, that we will proceed with this book under the premise that we all embrace the certainty of the age of innocence, prior to being held eternally accountable for sin. Hence, the purpose of this book is to better understand what that term means and, more importantly, what ages are included in this wonderful period of grace we know as the age of innocence. That is the period we all enjoyed prior to the law coming into our lives... prior to that age of accountability.

To those few who hold there is no age of innocence, I would simply warn they need to better understand our God who is Love. Can anyone who personally knows our gracious God still believe that a baby, aborted in his or her mother's womb, will then spend eternity in Hell because they, though unborn, are accountable for their sin nature? Or the precious soul born a month prematurely and does not survive will now suffer the torments of Hell because of their sin nature? To know God is to know of His love and grace. Perhaps those who do not believe in an age of innocence have not genuinely experienced the saving and forgiving grace of our Savior, cannot really understand it for others, and need to be saved immediately. Let us go on with our study...

God has seen fit, in His wondrous grace and love, to open the window of understanding on this age of innocence when He goes to a great length recording the loss of David's first son with Bathsheba in II Samuel 12:1-24. Please carefully read this portion in light of our subject on the age of accountability.

2 Sa 12:1-24, *"And the LORD sent Nathan unto David. And he came unto him, and said unto him, There were two men in one city; the one rich, and the other poor. The rich man had exceeding many flocks and herds: But the poor man had nothing, save one little ewe lamb, which he had bought and nourished up: and it grew up together with him, and with his children; it did eat of his own meat, and drank of his own cup, and lay in his bosom, and was unto him as a daughter. And there came a traveller unto the rich man, and he spared to take of his own flock and of his own herd, to dress for the wayfaring man that was come unto him; but took the poor man's lamb, and dressed it for the man that was come to him.*

Comfort ye, comfort ye my people, saith your God.

– Isaiah 40:1

And David's anger was greatly kindled against the man; and he said to Nathan, As the LORD liveth, the man that hath done this thing shall surely die: And he shall restore the lamb fourfold, because he did this thing, and because he had no pity. And Nathan said to David, Thou art the man. Thus saith the LORD God of Israel, I anointed thee king over Israel, and I delivered thee out of the hand of Saul; And I gave thee thy master's house, and thy master's wives into thy bosom, and gave thee the house of Israel and of Judah; and if that had been too little, I would moreover have given unto thee such and such things. Wherefore hast thou despised the commandment of the LORD, to do evil in his sight? thou hast killed Uriah the Hittite with the sword, and hast taken his wife to be thy wife, and hast slain him with the sword of the children of Ammon. Now therefore the sword shall never depart from thine house; because thou hast despised me, and hast taken the wife of Uriah the Hittite to be thy wife. Thus saith the LORD, Behold, I will raise up evil against thee out of thine own house, and I will take thy wives before thine eyes, and give them unto thy neighbour, and he shall lie with thy wives in the sight of this sun. For thou didst it secretly: but I will do this thing before all Israel, and before the sun. And David said unto Nathan, I have sinned against the LORD. And Nathan said unto David, The LORD also hath put away thy sin; thou shalt not die. Howbeit, because by this deed thou hast given great occasion to the enemies of the LORD to blaspheme, the child also that is born unto thee shall surely die. And Nathan departed unto his house. And the LORD struck the child that Uriah's wife bare unto David, and it was very sick. David therefore besought God for the child; and David fasted, and went in, and lay all night upon the earth. And the elders of his house arose, and went to him, to raise him up from the earth: but he would not, neither did he eat bread with them. And it came to pass on the seventh day, that the child died. And the servants of David feared to tell him that the child was dead: for they said, Behold, while the child was yet alive, we spake unto him, and he would not hearken unto our voice: how will he then vex himself, if we tell him that the child is dead? But when David saw that his servants whispered, David perceived that the child was dead: therefore David said unto his servants, Is the child dead? And they said, He is dead. Then David arose from the earth, and washed, and anointed himself, and changed his apparel, and came into the house of the LORD, and worshipped: then he came to his own house; and when he required, they set bread before him, and he did eat. Then said his servants unto him, What thing is this that thou hast done? thou didst fast and weep for the child, while it was alive; but when the child was dead, thou didst rise and eat bread. And he said, While the child was yet alive, I fasted and wept: for I said, Who can tell whether GOD will be gracious to me, that the child may live? But now he is dead, wherefore should I fast? can I bring him back again? I shall go to him, but he shall not return to me. And David comforted Bathsheba his wife, and went in unto her, and lay with her: and she bare a son, and he called his name Solomon: and the LORD loved him."

We need to keep in mind that this infant son was born out of a sinful relationship; the child seemingly has no name, and dies before any religious ceremony would have been performed over him. This child dies in his seventh day of life and dies as a direct judgment of God for the sins of David. A Jewish child would have been circumcised on the eighth day of life and at that point would be given his name. This is all significant because it is, in a sense, a "worst case scenario". God wants us to see that His grace is still greater than all our sins and all our circumstances. He wants mankind to understand there is a period of time when our sin nature will not condemn us to Hell. It is a space of time when we are not held eternally accountable to God, for either our sins or our sin nature. So we here have the presence of an age of immunity, an age of non-accountability, an age of being exempt from the eternal penalty of sin. This is also a subtle reminder that no religious ceremony can ever qualify us for eternity in heaven. This is only based on the grace of God.

It is enlightening to read of the actions of the father, King David, when he faces the reality that his son has now died. There is nothing left for him to do or even pray about and so he goes back to his great responsibilities as the king of Israel. Those in places of responsibility must often set aside emotions, problems, and situations and simply get back to work. But God will show us more...much more. **2 Sa 12:24a,** *"And David comforted Bathsheba his wife...".* These words did, in fact, bring her much comfort. She was so comforted that life was able to go back to normal immediately. **2 Samuel 12:24,** *"And David comforted Bathsheba his wife, and went in unto her, and lay with her: and she bare a son, and he called his name Solomon: and the LORD loved him."* Through this comfort she escaped depression. She understood and trusted God even in this difficult time. Ask yourself could David have comforted his wife by telling her "Only God knows where the child is right now"? Or, would she have been comforted by being told they will visit his grave once a month or once a week? of course not - he had to have shared with her the same wonderful truth he had shared with his staff. That this lifeless form lying before them was no longer their son. It was a mere empty container, a vessel, that once held their son. Their son was now in Heaven and though he would not come back to them, one day they would be with him in Heaven. **2 Co 1:3-4,** *"Blessed be God, even the Father of our Lord Jesus Christ, the Father of mercies, and the God of all comfort; Who comforteth us in all our tribulation, that we may be able to comfort them which are in any trouble, by the comfort wherewith we ourselves are comforted of God."*

We are unable to comfort others until we are comforted. We cannot be comforted unless we understand the Scriptures properly. So, there must be a biblical answer to the questions concerning the age of accountability and the age of innocence.

Chapter 3

Different Views

I do not wish to linger on the subject of different views. It is always better to study truth rather than error. If we fully understand truth, all error will be exposed. The only reason I took on the project of writing a book on this doctrinal truth is because there is so little written on the subject and so little understood by those who need it the most. If you have come this far into the book you are already challenged by how little you have been instructed on this subject and how little you personally know concerning this all-important doctrine. And you must ask yourself: those things you think you know on this subject, what are they based upon? And, most importantly, how specific is your understanding? What ages are involved, and is it possible to even know the answer to that question?

There are but two views on the overall subject. There either is an age of innocence or there is not an age of innocence. In case you have randomly opened the book to this page without reading the previous pages let me explain again the "age of innocence". The age of innocence is a period in everyone's life when he or she will not be held eternally accountable for their sins before God. The age of accountability, on the other hand, is the period of one's life when they **are** held eternally accountable for all their sins and must accept Christ and His finished work on Calvary to have forgiveness of those sins.

The first and clearly unacceptable "theory" is that there is no age of innocence and hence the age of accountability begins at conception. I hesitate to use space in this book to acknowledge such an understanding of our God. The very thought that the untold millions of unborn children that have been slaughtered through the sinful act of of abortion will spend eternity in Hell should be beyond the ability of a child of God to fathom. Because this view is so unchristian, so unreasonable and so unbiblical, I do not give it any additional space in this book.

The second and most widely accepted view, is that there is an age of innocence. Within this second view we find little agreement or even understanding as to what the doctrine teaches concerning the details of this special time in a person's life. Those who embrace this truth are correct in that they acknowledge the love and grace of God and teach that there is an age of innocence. So far as I can determine, anyone who subscribes to this view will agree that this age begins at

All scripture is given by inspiration of God, and is profitable for doctrine, for reproof, for correction, for instruction in righteousness:

– 2 Timothy 3:16

conception. From this one common denominator there seems to be little or no agreement as to when that age ends. And therein lies the problem. How do you teach a doctrine that seems to have only a beginning but no ending, a start but no finish? Most accept, without question, that there is an age of innocence and that this age begins at conception. Most cling to this important doctrine, with little or no Scripture to justify what it is they say they believe as to when that child does become accountable. If you do not understand this subject, how then can you ever bring comfort to yourself or others when a child or young person has been taken so unexpectedly?

Sadly, the only agreement seems to be that no one can know for sure when this age of innocence ends. They simply accept it as a Bible mystery. Some say it ends "around" **the age of five** (with no biblical basis whatsoever). Others like to point to Jesus going to the Temple at **the age of twelve** to somehow link the biblical reason to choose twelve as the age one steps into an eternally accountable state. Along with this trip to Jerusalem they love to bring in multiple religious traditions such as the unbiblical first communion and even the Jewish bat mitzvah and bar mitzvah as reasons to stand on twelve as the "approximate" age. Overwhelmingly however, most will say **it depends on the child**. It will depend on the maturity of the child and the upbringing in the home: were they taught the Scriptures at home, attended Sunday School, brought up in a Christian home? Somehow there is a thought developed that depending on the amount of spiritual light a child has been exposed to, then the age of accountability will descend on them more or less quickly. All of this is foreign to the Holy Scriptures.

Then we come to the purpose of this book, the biblically-based belief that this age of accountability does not begin until a person reaches twenty years of age. Yes, twenty!! I can say this only because that is what we will see over and over in Scripture. The unborn child is seen as not accountable, the children going through their "terrible twos" are not accountable. The difficult adolescent years and yes, even throughout the troubled and rebellious teen years: blameless, guiltless and mercifully exempted from God's eternal judgement. They are innocent in God's sight though they be sinners sinning on a daily basis: sinners but not accountable, sinning yet not accountable. They have all been given, as it were, "diplomatic immunity".

The chapters that follow are submitted to benefit both you and those who you may one day minister to in a very powerful and unexpected way.

When you first read "twenty years of age" your response was likely "No way- how is that possible?" You may have gasped and reread the paragraph. You may have even said to yourself (or called your spouse over and read it aloud to them, then said, "We can't know that!"). To which I must point out a verse we normally use only for those who have trusted Christ, but is applicable to those in the age of innocence: *"And this is the record, that God hath given to us eternal life, and this life is in his Son. He that hath the Son hath life; and he that hath not the Son of God hath not life. These things have I written unto you that believe on the name of the Son of God; that ye may know that ye have eternal life, and that ye may believe on the name of the Son of God."* 1Jn 5:11-13

"**Knowing**" means we should be able to say, with authority, that we know God's plan of grace and salvation from conception to death. We need to know exactly what we can tell a five-year-old, eleven-year-old, thirteen-year-old. But, if a child is thirteen and our understanding is that we cannot know when the age of accountability begins, then we can only say to that child, "I don't know" - prior to their accepting Christ. In this line of thinking, David could not have "known" where his son was and that one day he would go to him. Biblically, I believe that twenty is the age and this will be supported, verse by verse, throughout the Scriptures.

In addition to what I see as the irrefutable truth **throughout Scripture** of twenty years being the beginning of the age of accountability, we will also see this truth in **God's creation:** His intelligent design in how our development matches His mercy, grace and this doctrine. This is an exciting and unexpected discovery that helps us see the balance of this spiritual truth in our physical and psychological growth.

Chapter 4

Considering the Law of First Mention

Many of our homes, studies and offices are filled with commentaries. We often (much to our shame) spend more time reading books about the Bible than we spend reading the Bible. We spend more time studying authors than we spend studying Scriptures. Somewhere there must be a balance. I have spent twenty years thinking about, studying, and questioning the age of innocence and the age of accountability. I feel God has laid this important and neglected doctrine on my heart. There are no books written on this subject. I have searched for years: nothing! With no other books written on this subject my conclusions were arrived at from an unbiased searching of the Scriptures to see what God has to say on the subject. Now retired from full time pastoring, I have made this book, and the truth concerning the age of accountability my primary focus.

It would seem every biblical subject has been debated, argued and written on for 2,000 years. Yet, when I typed "the age of accountability" into the search engine of the largest book seller in the world, I found nothing. No book seems to exist on the subject. If I type in "the age of accountability" into a web search engine, I see 129,000,000 results, yet no one has seen the need to study the subject enough to actually publish a book on this doctrine.

I am reminded over and over that the average Christian and the average pastor has no idea of either the importance of this subject, or what they believe on this subject. Surprisingly, most Christians seem perfectly content being ignorant, or as the Bible calls it, willingly ignorant of it. Over the years I have found that Christians seem afraid of the subject, afraid that it might complicate their already established definition of salvation, or afraid people might use it as a ticket to sin...God forbid! They are afraid that sceptics might think it is "something new under the sun" when in fact it goes all the way back to the very beginning of the teachings of Exodus and is consistent throughout the Scriptures. We find no exceptions to explain away this marvelous doctrine in either the Old or the New Testaments. As we find with all true doctrine, it is consistent.

Every one that passeth among them that are numbered, from twenty years old and above, shall give an offering unto the LORD.

– Exo 30:14

We ought never to fear knowledge and never fear truth. Real knowledge and truth will always help us. When I was about sixteen years old, my friend and I would go bowling every Saturday morning. We were extremely competitive and loved that our scores had greatly improved over the years, though we seemed to have hit a bit of a plateau. On one occasion, or two, we each had even broken 200. We were feeling particularly good about ourselves. One Saturday, I will never forget, we were bowling and the man next to us was hitting strike after strike. After some time, he walked over to us and said he had been watching us and would help us if we would like. He gave us his name and explained that he was a professional bowler. We were excited until he started helping us. He explained that we were off on our basics: where we stood, how we approached and what we were aiming for. Then he said this, "If you start doing this the way I show you, your game will drop a bit at first, but over time you will greatly improve. If you choose to continue the way you are going, you will always be a fair bowler." We both incorporated his instruction and both of us, over time (after dropping a bit), greatly improved. I have remembered that wisdom now for over fifty years. I desire knowledge and wisdom on a daily basis. We can never settle for "fair" when God desires us to have "perfect" knowledge.

The truths I have learned while researching this amazing doctrine have helped me in many ways: how I see God's grace, how I interact with both young and older people, how I view the years we have with our children and our grandchildren. And most importantly, in seeing the complete picture of law, grace, truth and salvation.

What is the Law of First Mention?

The "law of first mention" is a widely accepted idea that the first time God reveals a word, a thought, a concept or even a doctrine in Scripture, the way it is used this first time will help you understand that word or truth each time you find it throughout the Bible. Using the first mention as our basis, our understanding will grow as we study this truth throughout Scripture. I mentioned commentaries lining our shelves... dictionaries both secular as was well as biblical also help us as we read and study God's Word. But, the law of first mention teaches us that the Bible will interpret and define words and concepts when first introduced often saving us the need to look them up in a commentary.

Because the purpose of this book is to focus on one doctrine, the age of accountability, I cannot take the time here to develop the law of first mention but to simply use the truth of that law to help us better understand our study on the age of accountability.

Applying the law of first mention to the phrase in Scripture "...**from** twenty years old..." we begin to see God's view of when man becomes responsible for his actions. This all-important phrase is first found in Scripture in **Ex 30:14** *"Every one that passeth among them that are numbered, from twenty years old and above, shall give an offering unto the LORD."* This is so important because this phrase, which is found twenty-seven times throughout the Bible, will be defined for us here. No other specific age is repeated as often and clearly; no other age in Scripture has the significance that twenty carries with it. The only age that comes even close would be "...**from thirty years old**" which is generally a reference for the priests of the Levites; an age that pertains to one being in a spiritual leadership roll or in a teaching position. As Scripture goes on, we see the consistency of this teaching as Jesus was thirty when He began His earthly ministry. Most

Bible commentators estimate Timothy to be thirty to thirty-five years when Paul says to him (referring to his ministry), in **I Timothy 4:12**, *"...let no man despise thy youth."* When the blind man was healed, and the Jewish leaders asked questions so they could punish someone, they asked the parents what had happened. The parents refused to answer but rather we find in **John 9:23**, *"Therefore said his parents, He is of age; ask him."* Most Bible teachers seem to agree that "full age" was considered to be thirty. This gives us a clearer understanding of God's timeline for maturity.

Let's take a few minutes to dissect **Exodus 30:14** and understand it within its context. *"Every one that passeth among them that are numbered, from twenty years old and above, shall give an offering unto the LORD."*

<u>Every one that passeth among them</u> – "every one" - We are looking at a group of people, an all-inclusive group of people. The purpose of this verse alone, as well as in its context, is to give the entire group (**every one**) specific instruction on how to make a subgroup from that group. In essence, it is describing a group within the larger group that will be accountable or required to do something. In this case it requires the subgroup to give an offering unto the LORD. But those specifically excluded are not required to give this same offering that **every one** is to give.

<u>...that are numbered,</u> - Throughout Scripture you have to appreciate the way that God talks to us like we are children. He will say something one way, then immediately say it again another way and sometimes even a third time all in an effort for us to understand what He is saying. And still we seem not to get it. First He says **"every one"** and now He says **"..that are numbered"**. You look at a group and then you want to count the number of people. But God says I want you to count every one of them, but of the **"every one"** in the group, the people who you actually count must be within a certain age requirement.

<u>...from twenty years old and above,</u> - Here are the guidelines for counting the children of Israel. From the time they reach their twentieth birthday and then for the rest of their life, they will be counted. God is speaking to Moses at this time and for the first time in world history He is dividing mankind into two distinct groups: young and old, mature and immature, responsible and not responsible, accountable and not accountable or innocent and guilty. But for what?...

<u>...shall give an offering unto the LORD.</u> – They were simply to give an offering to the LORD. Already this does not make sense to our twenty-first century mentality. Why doesn't an eighteen-year-old need to give an offering? Why not

a sixteen-year-old? Once again, without Scripture, we would be arguing and questioning, year by year, about when should our children start giving such an offering. We would think a pastor's child would be ok, because of having been taught; he or she would be expected to give an offering before a child that rides in on the bus. But the one fact we know from this verse is that, in this instance, at this moment in history, God spoke to Moses with a very specific command. If a person is twenty years of age or older, they give the offering. If they have not yet reached their twentieth birthday...they are not to give the offering. Period. But...what if they are nineteen?...No! Raised in the home of a priest?...No! A high priest?...No!

In the next verse there is further clarification on the matter of this offering. The offering includes **EVERY ONE** rich and poor alike. Ex **30:15a**, *"The rich shall not give more, and the poor shall not give less than half a shekel, when they give an offering unto the LORD,..."* Everyone gives the offering and the offering must be identical. The rich do not pay more and the poor do not pay less. All are equal before the Lord. It seems safe to say that the rich and the poor who have given their offering and those under the age of twenty are all equal in God's sight at that point. A twelve-year-old who did not give the offering was not in trouble with Moses or God. He or she has done all that was requested and/or required by the Lord of them at that time in their lives.

This brings us to what may be the most interesting part of this whole account, the first mention of "...twenty years old and above...". We need to ask ourselves "What is the offering for?" The end of **Exodus 30:15** tells us exactly what it is for. *"...to make an atonement for your souls."* Ellicott says of this Scripture:

> "On being formally **enrolled** among the people of God, it would be brought home to every man how unworthy he was of such favour, how necessary it was that atonement should in some way or other be made for him. God therefore appointed a way—the same way for all—in order to teach strongly that all souls were of equal value in His sight, and that **unworthiness**, whatever its degree, required the same expiation." (Emphasis by author, because "all" did not begin until twenty years of age).

So, using Ellicott's understanding of this portion of Scripture, **every one** would be "worthy" who needed to be "made" worthy. Those under age twenty were not required to do anything to become "worthy".

Israel soon began their forty years of wilderness experiences following the offering made for the atonement of all. Yet we just read that this offering only pertained to those twenty years of age and older. Was God not "merciful" to **all** the children of Israel? Were the children who did not give an offering for the atonement of their souls also allowed to eat of the manna, drink of the water? Of course they were. God was merciful to them throughout their journeys without having made "atonement" for their souls, without an atonement being made for them. They were not cleansed, disannulled, purged or reconciled...yet, God was merciful to them.

Keep in mind this is only the first mention of this age of twenty and upward. But it does give us the essence of understanding that when God looks at His creation, when He sees mankind, they are divided - young and old. The old were accountable for something while the young were not accountable for the same transgression. Those under twenty years of age were still under His mercy. Remember this age will be referred to twenty-six more times in Scripture. This is simply the first mention. But back to this occurrence...

We have looked at **Exodus 30:15** where the offering is *"...to make an <u>atonement</u> for your souls"*. This verse is a confirmation and is building upon what God had already told Moses in **Ex 30:12**, *"When thou takest the sum of the children of Israel after their number, then shall they give every man <u>a ransom for his soul</u> unto the LORD, when thou numberest them; that there be no plague among them, when thou numberest them."*.

In Exodus 30:12 God tells Moses **"every man"**. There is no explanation from God concerning this specific age because it would seem that to Moses and to all of Israel the age of being responsible was already understood to be twenty years of age. It was for our benefit that God included that statement in Exodus 30:14; God uses His Word to give us clarity. It is "line upon line, precept upon precept". He does the same thing with the purpose of the offering. Two separate words in Exodus 30:12 and Exodus 30:15 are used to make clear the importance of the offering. While this offering is especially important, it is required only from those twenty years of age and older. In Exodus 30:12 God tells us the offering is for the *"ransom* (kopher – redemption, ransom, satisfaction) *of his soul"*. Then just three verses later, in Exodus 30:15 God describes it as making an *"atonement* (kaphar – to placate, cancel, appease, cleanse, forgive, pacify, pardon, purge and reconcile.) *for your souls"*. Yet, those under twenty do not need to be ransomed, cleansed or even forgiven.

Considering the Law of First Mention

When we look at the meaning of these words and move them into the New Testament we have no problem seeing a picture of salvation through Jesus Christ. "Forgive, reconcile, purge, redemption, ransom..." as we move these terms and responsibilities to the New Testament, we must bring with them the whole counsel of God. Who exactly was it that needed to be ransomed? Only those who were twenty years of age and older were "under the Law". Paul speaks of being alive *"without the Law once"* which was prior to reaching his twentieth birthday: but then the Law "came, sin revived, and I died" following reaching the age of accountability. **Romans 7:9** *"For I was alive without the law once: but when the commandment came, sin revived, and I died".* Again, this is only the first mention...so much more to come.

Chapter 5

Biblical Age for Military Service

God set a specific age for those who could serve in the military. *"From twenty years old and upward..."* One of the disconcerting arguments I have heard against the age of twenty for accountability before God (and I have experienced it multiple times) is when someone says to me, "Well if you can join the military when you are eighteen (even seventeen with parental consent) you should be accountable to God for your sins". It is funny how we are so in tune with the world that when confronted with God's Word our first inclination is to quote what our government does. Personally, what I find most amazing is that, today, Israel drafts their young people at eighteen years of age when Old Testament scriptures make it abundantly clear that only those *"from twenty years old and upward..."* were **"able"** to go to war. **Num 1:3** *"From twenty years old and upward, all that are able to go forth to war in Israel: thou and Aaron shall number them by their armies".*

All those over the age of twenty would be counted and considered **eligible** to go to war, **able** to go to war. No one before that age was considered **"able"** to go and should not be considered. An eighteen- or nineteen-year-old would never be considered **"able"** to go to war. Think about that. The vast majority of young people seventeen-, eighteen-, or nineteen-years-olds are MORE than physically **able** to join the military and to go to war. They go through boot camp like it is a walk in the park. As we get older the physical drain of service becomes more and more difficult and I am aware of the physical cost. This author served for twenty years active duty so I am well aware of the physical cost of military life. And, as a recruiter for twelve of those twenty years I can also tell you that those between the ages of seventeen and nineteen are the most enthusiastic about going into the military. They actually look forward to going - even into war. Oddly enough, if you go down to twelve or sixteen-year-olds, they see it as glamorous, and the closer to the front lines...the more glamorous it seems. They often wish they could join at their current age and see no reason why leaving school and family should not be allowed.

From twenty years old and upward, all that are able to go forth to war in Israel: thou and Aaron shall number them by their armies.

– Numbers 1:3

Would you like to see the age for military service dropped to twelve? You gasp and are justifiably appalled at the very thought, yet you accept that twelve is an appropriate age to be ready, expected, required, and mandated, by God, to either be enlisted into His army or condemned to Hell if that decision is not made by twelve years of age. Prior to reading this book, you would say that twelve is plenty old enough for a person to consider their sinful condition and make a decision for Christ (While I 100% agree that a twelve-year-old is fully capable of trusting Christ it is not mandated by God at such a young age). Many would go far beyond the simple ability to accept Christ at this young age and think it **mandatory** that they be ready for eternity to come, that they are mandatorily accountable to their Creator God for their actions. How does one come up with that arbitrary age? Let me ask you this: what would you think if the age to be married was dropped to twelve, or even eight - again, a ridiculous concept! You might say, "No eight or twelve-year-old is ready to make a decision that will affect the rest of their life." Oh, but you do believe that God will make it mandatory that by that age they have to have made the decision to turn to Christ for salvation and will already have done so...or else! In fact, most people vaguely believe that one has only till about five years of age before they are 100% accountable for their sins. How can we so easily dismiss a lack of maturity for marriage and military while at the same time not see it in the importance of eternal matters?

Another parallel is that some, in years past, did in fact get married at twelve and fifteen and lived happily ever after. But would we ever make a law that said you MUST be married by twelve? No! In fact, we have made laws that say you absolutely cannot make that lifelong decision at that young and tender age. It is actually against our laws to get married, anywhere, at that age. I want to make something abundantly clear at this point. Though I believe the Scriptures do not hold man eternally accountable until they are twenty years of age, I see this period of time as a glorious showing of the grace and mercy of God. It is a time that allows us to mature, grow, and in the case of those not brought up in a Christian environment, a time to even seek for truth. One can be saved any time during those first nineteen years of life but he or she will not be held accountable for their sins and their sin nature until they reach the age of accountability which Scripture repeatedly shows to be age twenty. I do not want to be misunderstood for thinking a child is not capable of understanding their sinful condition and not able to simply receive Christ as their Savior. They are able, they are expected to do this in God's sight, and many are saved at a very young age. But, again, God in his infinite mercy and grace has given them time to figure it out and to act on what they have learned.

So as not to appear to be picking out only certain Scriptures that fit into the book, fifteen times we find the matter of age twenty being the minimum age requirement for a person in Israel to be considered for military service. Fifteen of the twenty-seven times the phrase is used it is used to show how an eighteen-year-old or a nineteen-year-old is not **emotionally** or psychologically ready for military service. How can that be? I am glad you asked. This too will be answered in a chapter to come.

One of the verses of particular interest concerning the age of those to go into battle is 2 Ch 25:5 *"Moreover Amaziah gathered Judah together, and made them captains over thousands, and captains over hundreds, according to the houses of their fathers, throughout all Judah and Benjamin: and he numbered them from twenty years old and above, and found them three hundred thousand choice men, able to go forth to war, that could handle spear and shield."*

Finding this same phrase so far along in Israel's history demonstrates the already accepted guidelines of generals, as well as kings, that God had set standards which could never be broken. In **2 Chronicles 25:5** we see that it was King Amaziah who numbered the people for war but refused to number them if they were under the age of twenty. Please note it is Amaziah who receives one of the few positive reviews in God's report when it is recorded in **2 Ch 25:2**, *"And he did that which was <u>right</u> in the sight of the LORD, but not with a perfect heart"*. Though his heart was not always right, he did obey the "letter of the law". It seems Amaziah was a stickler for details, for the letter of the law as seen again in **2 Ch 25:3-4**, *"Now it came to pass, when the kingdom was established to him, that he slew his servants that had killed the king his father. <u>But he slew not their children, but did as it is written in the law in the book of Moses,</u> where the LORD commanded, saying, The fathers shall not die for the children, neither shall the children die for the fathers, but every man shall die for his own sin."* Clearly Amaziah understood accountability from God's Word and followed it to the very letter. He saw the children as not being accountable for any transgressions.

In the next verse, following God's recognition of Amaziah's obedience to His Word concerning the accountability of sons and fathers toward each other's sins, we find he is also obedient in not counting children to be considered for war. I use the word **"children"** at this point to help us begin to see that, in God's eyes, those under twenty years of age are, in fact, children. Perhaps not by the definition we use today, but by God's definition they are children. They are children in God's sight as we see those who are twenty years of age and older now referred to as "men". In **2 Ch 25:5** we are told that Amaziah *"...found them three hundred thousand choice men...".* Not only are they <u>men</u> but they are **"<u>able</u> to go forth to war,..."** (again underlining for emphasis). Here is where we begin to better understand why those who are younger are not "able" to go to war while those who are older are considered able. It is not a physical limitation but rather, emotionally and psychologically they are not ready for battle. If they are not emotionally and psychologically ready to go to war to risk their physical life how can we arbitrarily feel they are old enough in God's eyes to be drafted, and forced into the reality of eternity?

Part of that answer to the question of why those under twenty are not "able" to go to war can be found in the close of **2 Ch 25:5** *"...men, able to go forth to war, <u>that could handle spear and shield</u>."* It would be an unusual sixteen, seventeen, eighteen and certainly nineteen-year-old who would not be strong enough, agile enough, and excited enough, to pick up, and physically handle both a spear and a shield. We must consider the word used here, **"handle"**. This is a most interesting word and needs to be understood to accept God's command that a nineteen-year-old cannot go into battle. "Handle" (Heb, achaz) has the simple understanding of a question of ability to pick up and use a piece of equipment, but it also means to **"be affrighted"**. Herein lies the pivotal point of our understanding. A teenager knows no fear. They do not fully understand the finality of war, the real horrors of war even when they have been told them, shown them and warned about them. In short...they do not mentally, emotionally, or spiritually understand **consequences**.

While on one hand a young person may not be affrighted to go headlong into battle, there is another whole group that would not be emotionally prepared to take the life of another. We see this, perhaps, in the life of Gideon when he orders his son, Jether, to slay Zebah and Zalmunna for killing Gideon's brothers, Jether's uncles. We are told that Jether refused to kill them. God, in His Word, gives us not the excuse, but the reason Jether did not obey his father. In **Judges 8:20** we are told, *"...But the youth drew not his sword; for he feared, <u>because</u> he was yet a youth."* Interestingly, we are not told if he feared drawing his sword, feared taking a life, or feared going against God's age command. We are not told exactly what age Jether was, but we are told because of his youth he did not obey.

What goes through a young mind when they put on a bed sheet and jump from a garage roof? Then, years later, these same young people take their skateboard (while refusing to wear a helmet) down a cement stairway handrail and somehow think nothing could possibly go wrong. Others ride their bicycles as fast as they can toward some homemade ramp thinking they will somehow go airborne and land safely on the other side. They all do these things because they do not understand **consequences**. Nothing "frightens" them. They do not think it will be their head that gets injured. Young people rush into war never imagining that they could be the one who dies, is wounded, or is permanently disabled.

Statistics show the average age of someone trying their first cigarette is at age eighteen. This is because they do not conceive the idea of the consequences of that single action. The Betty Ford Foundation posted recently that "It is believed sixteen is the pivotal year for adolescents, who face increasing peer pressure to experiment with drugs and alcohol, while being 'afforded a greater degree of adult status by their parents'. After eighteen, risks for alcohol and marijuana decline and by age twenty-two the risk has nearly ended." Do you not find it more than coincidental that these ages fall so closely in agreement with the biblical ages we have been exploring?

We will explore this phenomenon of young people and their lack of understanding consequences much more in a chapter to come. It is important for you, at this point, to begin to see that it is by the grace and mercy of God that He gives His created beings time to hear, seek, understand and then, most importantly, consider the consequences of obeying or not obeying the Gospel.

Chapter 6

Biblical View of Levitical Service

David's son died and David comforted his wife with the truth that their son was not eternally accountable for his sins or even his sin nature and that one day they would see him again in Heaven. When David counted his people for war, he counted only those who were of the age of twenty and above because those younger were not responsible to fight the wars. God wanted only those who He considered "men" to fight. When the offering was taken for the atonement and the ransom of sins God specifically exempted those who were under twenty years of age as they needed neither atonement nor the ransom for their sins. They were not to be responsible for this offering.

For the most part everyone accepts that David's seven-day-old son was not going to be held eternally accountable for His sins or his sin nature and would readily agree that David and Bathsheba are enjoying eternity with him today. If someone believes that this seven-day-old child is in Hell, they would need to question their understanding of God's grace. Or they would have to assume that David is in Hell today with him because he knew he would be with his son in eternity. But if you understand me to say that even if his child had been nineteen, he is still in Heaven then perhaps you were upset with such an "advanced" age (I say "were" in hopes you are beginning to see the truth of this advanced age of accountability). After all, he is old enough to fight in the United States military! Yes, but in the case of David's army, God says not "able" to fight. The problem always comes back to: when does that age of not being responsible, that age of "innocence" really end? When does God begin to hold man eternally accountable for their sins? Even as we work our way through these Bible truths you may tend to recoil from the older age of twenty. No one is able to defend an earlier age with Scripture, but the older age does not seem right to our modern-day thinking. I will not say that this truth is pivotal to everything that we believe. But I will say this: we do not fully understand the extent of the love and grace of God until we accept this Bible truth. And I will say, the first time a grieving parent approaches you with a loss of their teenager, you will be very thankful that you fully understand this specific, no longer vague, biblical truth.

Now in the second year of their coming unto the house of God at Jerusalem, in the second month,... Zerubbabel...appointed the Levites, from twenty years old and upward, to set forward the work of the house of the LORD.

– Ezr 3:8

These chapters, so far, are only the foundation for the chapters yet to come. We are constructing a building of understanding. The amazing wording that God uses in the Old Testament to show the innocence of those under twenty years of age will, I believe, convince you of an older age of innocence. And then we will look at what the New Testament says about all this – it is exciting - there is no other word for it...EXCITING. May I even say, "life changing"? Stay with me as we lay yet another scriptural block to our foundation just before putting the walls of this truth up. From David, to war, to offerings for sins and now to temple service. Let us look at the next example of this common denominator of "...**from** twenty years old..." Here we see that God chose the Levites to be the priests for all Israel; but God only considers certain Levites "eligible" or even allowed to serve in any capacity in the house of the Lord.

God uses David, once again, to give this command, **1 Ch 23:27** *"For by the last words of David the Levites were numbered from twenty years old and above."* Whether going to war with shield and sword, or serving in the Temple, God saw man as two groups: responsible to serve and not responsible to serve, accountable or not accountable, able and not able, allowed and not allowed.

Read this truth within its context and its clarity and application to our subject of the age of accountability becomes clearer.

1Ch 23:24-32, *"These were the sons of Levi after the house of their fathers; even the chief of the fathers, as they were counted by number of names by their polls, that <u>did the work for the service of the house of the LORD, from the age of twenty years and upward.</u> For David said, The LORD God of Israel hath given rest unto his people, that they may dwell in Jerusalem for ever: And also unto the Levites; they shall no more carry the tabernacle, nor any vessels of it for the service thereof. For by the last words of David the Levites were numbered from <u>twenty years old and above:</u> Because <u>their office was to wait on the sons of Aaron for the service of the house of the LORD, in the courts, and in the chambers,</u> and in the purifying of all holy things, and the work of the service of the house of God; Both for the shewbread, and for the fine flour for meat offering, and for the unleavened cakes, and for that which is baked in the pan, and for that which is fried, and for all manner of measure and size; And to stand every morning to thank and praise the LORD, and likewise at even; And to offer all burnt sacrifices unto the LORD in the sabbaths, in the new moons, and on the set feasts, by number, according to the order commanded unto them, continually before the LORD: And that they should keep the charge of the tabernacle of the congregation, and the charge of the holy place, and the charge of the sons of Aaron their brethren, in the service of the house of the LORD."*

Looking at the portion of the Scripture which I have underlined, we see that young people were not even numbered as a "son of Levi" if they were under the age of twenty. Those under the age of twenty were not to serve in the Temple; they were not expected or even allowed to serve.

The example of Samuel

Think with me about Samuel. He was given to the Lord by his mother before he was ever born. He was taken to Eli and given to the Lord; we are told he *"ministered unto the Lord before Eli",* I Samuel 3:1. From his mother, Hannah, asking God for a "child" and throughout much of his time with Eli, Samuel is referred to over and over as…a **child.**

I Samuel:

1:11 *And she vowed a vow, and said, O LORD of hosts, if thou wilt indeed look on the affliction of thine handmaid, and remember me, and not forget thine handmaid, but wilt give unto thine handmaid a man child, then I will give him unto the LORD all the days of his life, and there shall no razor come upon his head.*

1:22 *But Hannah went not up; for she said unto her husband, I will not go up until the child be weaned, and then I will bring him, that he may appear before the LORD, and there abide for ever.*

1:24 *And when she had weaned him, she took him up with her, with three bullocks, and one ephah of flour, and a bottle of wine, and brought him unto the house of the LORD in Shiloh: and the child was young.*

1:25 *And they slew a bullock, and brought the child to Eli.*

1:27 *For this child I prayed; and the LORD hath given me my petition which I asked of him:*

2:11 *And Elkanah went to Ramah to his house. And the child did minister unto the LORD before Eli the priest.*

2:18 *But Samuel ministered before the LORD, being a child, girded with a linen ephod.*

2:21 *And the LORD visited Hannah, so that she conceived, and bare three sons and two daughters. And the child Samuel grew before the LORD.*

2:26 *And the child Samuel grew on, and was in favour both with the LORD, and also with men.*

3:1 *And the child Samuel ministered unto the LORD before Eli. And the word of the LORD was precious in those days; there was no open vision.*

3:8 *And the LORD called Samuel again the third time. And he arose and went to Eli, and said, Here am I; for thou didst call me. And Eli perceived that the LORD had called the child.*

For the first three chapters we see a young man growing and preparing to serve God. But over and over he is referred to as a "child"...not yet ready. We might even say not yet permitted to do the things he would one day be called on to do. After God's clear calling in the life of Samuel, God tells us that Samuel would still need to grow, mature and learn. We are told in **1Sa 3:19**, *"And Samuel grew, and the LORD was with him, and did let none of his words fall to the ground."*

Samuel continued as a young person to prepare himself. He was not the only one who knew one day he would be a prophet of God. We have already seen that in **I Samuel 3:8**, *"...Eli perceived that the LORD had called the child."* Now we see in **I Sa 3:20**, *"And all Israel from Dan even to Beersheba knew that Samuel was established to be a prophet of the LORD."* We learn from Strong's Concordance that this word "established", in the Hebrew "aman", means "to build up or support; to foster as a parent or nurse." Again, we see Samuel was but a child (though we know he was at minimum thirteen years of age at this point) and though called while a child, not yet placed into service. He was learning, growing, and preparing for the day he would be activated into full-time service.

After Samuel was called, trained and matured, we see God used him to speak, as a prophet to Israel. **I Sa 4:1**, *"And the word of Samuel came to all Israel. Now Israel went out against the Philistines to battle, and pitched beside Ebenezer: and the Philistines pitched in Aphek,"* It is important to note that though Samuel is referred to eleven times as a child prior to this day, he will never be referred to as a child again.

As in all things, God can at any time he chooses use whomsoever He would like and whenever He would like. We are limited but He is not. If He speaks through a donkey, He can, through the mouths of babes, do great things. What we take note of is how things normally work throughout Scripture and that God does not generally send a boy to do a man's job. He does not place the responsibility of a man upon the shoulders of a boy, a child. But God being God, allowed David to defeat a giant and can do as He pleases in the workings of men. Our sovereign God can do as He pleases, but you and I must rely on His revealed Word to conduct our daily lives.

Chapter 7

The Exodus
The Spiritual Applications to This Truth

The Exodus is where I began this journey concerning the "age of accountability". Many years ago, while preaching a series, the "Wilderness Journeys" I saw God's perspective concerning men and children: between those who would be held accountable for their actions and those who would not be held accountable. And that difference was repeatedly and consistently twenty years of age and upward. If you have prayerfully read this far and are still uncertain, I believe your journey through the wilderness with the children of Israel will convince you. Their experiences with God should nudge you, even reluctantly, over the line to understanding. The subject of accountability is so unexplored that it has been relegated by many, to what we refer to as a Bible mystery. This word mystery in Scripture simply means something in Scripture that, at this time, cannot be known. It is interesting to note that though referred to as a mystery, many have developed their own dogmatic opinion on the subject. My challenge to you, as you read, is that if you did not have a biblically-based understanding of the age of accountability when you started this book, allow the Word of God to direct your understanding.

The children of Israel watched as God performed miracle after miracle in the land of Egypt. Plagues came and went like a perfectly choreographed ballet with Moses as the conductor and his staff the baton. These plagues play out, as they affect Egypt and the Egyptians, while exempting God's people over and over. Israel carried on like nothing happened, until that awful night when the horrible wailing of Egyptian mothers could be heard throughout all of Egypt...the sound that can only come from a mother who has lost a child far too early. Death came too quickly, too unexpectedly and Egypt now realized their losses were senseless and needless. To make it worse, it was not just any child, but their firstborn sons. Wailing could be heard in every Egyptian home, rich and poor, from the palace to the poorest. In stark contrast, these cries came to the ears of Jewish mothers as they shared the first Passover meal with their family safe and secure inside their blood-protected homes. They had their children sitting safely on their laps. The death angel had no power over them, all because of the blood. The death angel could do nothing because of God's mercy and grace toward them.

Moreover your little ones, which ye said should be a prey, and your children, which in that day had no knowledge between good and evil, they shall go in thither, and unto them will I give it, and they shall possess it.

– Deuteronomy 1:39

Imagine with me the scene in Pharaoh's home that terrible night. Pharaoh could not wait until morning. You can imagine the tone of voice as his wife tells him to do whatever it takes to end this battle with the God of Israel. She is standing there with their lifeless firstborn in her arms, giving Pharaoh no choice. "Let them go as Moses has asked"; she cries out, "NOW!" And so he does; he too has had enough. Angry and brokenhearted, he sends in the middle of the night to tell Moses and Aaron to pack up and leave. The unbelievable news spreads to all the children of Israel like wildfire. "...take your flocks and your herds, as ye have said, and be gone;..." The Egyptians willingly give them jewelry of silver and gold to help them along their way. All of Israel saw this, all of Israel enjoyed God's hand in this. And in **Ex 12:51** we are told, *"And it came to pass the selfsame day, that the LORD did bring the children of Israel out of the land of Egypt by their armies."*

As God personally began to guide Israel to their destination by either a cloud or a pillar of fire, they willingly followed the leading of God and Moses out of Egypt. All was well until they reached what seemed to be the impasse of the Red

Sea. Behind them the shock of death quickly faded from Pharaoh and his heart was hardened and hate mixed with anger, pride, and revenge took over. The most powerful army in the world pursued and bore down on defenseless Israel as they approached what seemed to be certain death on the banks of the Red Sea. Rather than trusting God the Israelites began to murmur, complain and regret that Moses had ever bothered them with this foolhardy dream of salvation, freedom and a promised land of their own. They wished he had just left them alone.

We fast-forward as all the people watched the Red Sea part before them. They crossed over on dry land, and wondered at God's omnipotence as the same sea that offered them life dealt only death to all the Egyptian army. From this miracle God went on to provide water miraculously, bread mysteriously, and the Law eternally etched on heart and now written on stone. Israel also watched as God's wrath was brought down on those who would make a false idol after all that they had seen. **Exodus 32:35,** *"And the LORD plagued the people, because they made the calf, which Aaron made."*

Once the tabernacle was built, they were ready for the next chapter of their new life. As a nation they were to go and claim a new land that was promised to flow with milk and honey **given** to them by God. As they arrived in Kadesh, they were as close as they could be to embracing the fulfillment of God's promise. Rather than living by faith and going in to claim the land they decided to form a committee and send in twelve spies to tell them whether they should or should not obey God. All Israel waited anxiously for their report. The report was beyond their wildest dreams and their darkest fears; this new land did, indeed, flow with milk and honey. Beyond milk and honey, one cluster of grapes took two men to carry and figs and pomegranates were plentiful. But there was one faith-shattering problem in the report of the committee of twelve. The group of twelve spies (one from each of the twelve tribes) gave their report, but they proceeded from reporting to opinions. The current occupants were truly giants and when the spies considered such a people they said, *"...we were in our own sight as grasshoppers, and so we were in their sight."* **Nu 13:33b**

As in most spiritual decisions this report was not unanimous. Among the twelve spies sent in for reconnaissance, ten came back with fear, doubt and a negative report. But two, Joshua and Caleb, saw the situation not through men's eyes, but more like David, who would one day see the giant of a man Goliath; they would see everything through God's eyes. They saw the threat through the filter and understanding of God's promises. When viewed through eyes of faith rather than eyes of fear, their only report could be like that of David's in years to come: when all the mighty warriors of Israel fell back in fear, a young shepherd, David said, in **1 Sam 17:26b** *"...who is this uncircumcised Philistine, that he should defy the armies of the living God?"*

We are told in Numbers 14 that Joshua and Caleb were distraught because of the report brought by the majority. They tore their clothing in distress, pointed out that the land promised to them by God Himself, was everything God told them it would be. They tried to convince the people that God would be pleased to bring them into the land. God would keep His promises if only they would not *"...rebel... against the LORD, neither fear ye the people of the land..."* **Nu 14:9b**

And now we come to the pivotal point of our study on the age of accountability. This is the point where we must start asking ourselves, "What does God mean by that?". "How does God see us from His omniscient view?" Look with me at **Numbers 14:1-4,** *"<u>And all the congregation</u> lifted up their voice, and cried; and the <u>people</u> wept that night. <u>And all the children of Israel murmured</u> against Moses and against Aaron: and <u>the whole congregation</u> said unto them, Would God that we had died in the land of Egypt! or would God we had died in this wilderness! And wherefore hath the LORD brought us unto this land, to fall by the sword, that our wives and our children should be a prey? were it not better for us to return into Egypt? And <u>they said</u> one to another, Let us make a captain, and let us return into Egypt."*.

What do you see? You must see that the opinion was unanimous! "Everyone" sided with the ten. We see that everyone had the opinion that they needed to turn around and go back to Egypt. They were angry with Moses, Joshua, Caleb and with God. To the point we read in Numbers **14:10a,** *"But <u>all the congregation</u> bade stone them with stones..."*. Everyone wanted Joshua and Caleb stoned for their opinion. At this point God showed them they had crossed a line they should never have crossed. God showed up in **Numbers 14:10b** *..."And the glory of the LORD appeared in the tabernacle of the congregation <u>before all the children of Israel</u>."*

Punishment for "all" who provoked God and did not trust Him is now proclaimed. Numbers 14:22-23, *"Because <u>all those men</u> which have seen my glory, and my miracles, which I did in Egypt and in the wilderness, and have tempted me now these ten times, and have not hearkened to my voice; Surely <u>they</u> shall not see the land which I sware unto their fathers, neither shall <u>any</u> of them that <u>provoked</u>*

me see it:" The people had crossed a line they should never have crossed. In unison they had rejected the miracles, the promises and the future that God had in store for them. In God's mercy, He uses men to deal with mankind. He speaks to men who can then take His message to man. He uses prophets, priests, judges, pastors, evangelists and here He used Moses.

God gives a message to Moses to give to all the people. **Numbers 14:26-33**, *"And the LORD spake unto Moses and unto Aaron, saying, How long shall I bear with this evil congregation, which murmur against me? I have heard the murmurings of the children of Israel, which they murmur against me. Say unto them, As truly as I live, saith the LORD, as ye have spoken in mine ears, so will I do to you: <u>Your carcases shall fall in this wilderness;</u> and <u>all that were numbered of you</u>, according to your whole number, <u>from twenty years old and upward</u>, which have murmured against me, Doubtless ye shall not come into the land, concerning which I sware to make you dwell therein, save Caleb the son of Jephunneh, and Joshua the son of Nun. But <u>your little ones</u>, which ye said should be a prey, them will I bring in, and they shall know the land which ye have despised. But as for you, your carcases, they shall fall in this wilderness. And <u>your children shall wander in the wilderness forty years</u>, and bear your whoredoms, until your carcases be wasted in the wilderness."*

In chapters three and four of this book we looked at the numbering of the people. The age of responsibility toward Israel in both war as well as the tabernacle service was twenty years old and upward. When we looked at the numbering of men for war and the age of twenty was drawn, there was no argument within the congregation. No debates shown among spiritual leaders or even secular leaders. It was a number, a figure, a concept that was completely understood and accepted by God's people. This specific age exception to the rules was not something that God had to explain or defend to His people. Like creation…it was simply known, accepted, and followed throughout Scripture. This people who loved to murmur and complain about most of God's plans, acquiesced to this age requirement without a word of complaint when they were told who should or should not serve in the military; who had or did not have a responsibility to the Temple for a tax for their soul…not a word. And now, the death sentence was handed down to "…all that were numbered". The definition of who is accountable for what they say and do and who is not accountable for what they say and do was apparently understood by all Israel. It was already understood but God would reiterate the guidelines of His kingdom. They were told again (and for our sakes) that **"everyone"** who had murmured against God's decision here would die in the wilderness and never see the promised land. But that "everyone" did not include a nineteen-year-old, or an eighteen-year-old...all the way down to the infants and even the unborn that would be born in the next nine months.

Have you ever known an eighteen-year-old without an opinion or a sixteen-year-old, or a thirteen-year-old? They all have opinions and they are very quick to voice them. Isn't that what we dread about our children reaching the teen years? Without a doubt, the young people were murmuring just like their parents...but they would not die in the wilderness with their parents. God explains why this is. Joshua and Caleb would go in because they, as adults, trusted Him and would be rewarded because of it. Those under twenty years of age he calls in **Numbers 14:31**, *"..your little ones..."* and in verse 33 *"..your children..."* They were not looked upon as adults and they were not going to be held accountable for what they said or did... though everyone twenty years of age and older certainly would be.

Look at yet another record of this truth and the wording that makes it even clearer for us. Moses says: **Deuteronomy 1:37-39** *Also the LORD was angry with me for your sakes, saying, Thou also shalt not go in thither. But Joshua the son of Nun, which standeth before thee, he shall go in thither: encourage him: for he shall cause Israel to inherit it. Moreover your <u>little ones,</u> which ye said should be a prey, <u>and your children, which in that day had no knowledge between good and evil,</u> they shall go in thither, and unto them will I give it, and they shall possess it.* So there it is. God's Word gives us the very definition we need. In God's sight, those under the age of twenty did not die in the wilderness because they did not have the "knowledge between good and evil". That is why they don't go into war, that is why they do not need to pay "a ransom for their soul". It does not mean they have never been taught, but that they are not yet at the place where God will hold them eternally accountable for their decisions. They do not understand the consequences of decisions between good and evil. We see this again in Isaiah 7:16 *For <u>before</u> the child <u>shall know</u> to refuse the evil, and choose the good, the land that thou abhorrest shall be forsaken of both her kings.*

Still not convinced? Though you may have picked up this book because you did not have any of the answers to the question of the age of accountability, you may still find it almost impossible to accept the Biblical answer because it rubs against all that you ever thought or believed concerning God's dealing with mankind. It has taken me two decades to take the thoughts I have concerning this subject, finally put them in writing, answer all of my own questions, and now to publish a book that I suspect may be somewhat controversial. That said, yes, there is still

The Exodus – *The Spiritual Applications to This Truth*

more; there is still much more on this subject. The New Testament saints completely understood this truth. The age of accountability is no more "taught" in the New Testament than is creation because it is an assumed understanding that this is simply the way God works. This truth was accepted by all of God's people throughout the Scriptures. Old Testament saints as well as New Testament believers understood this basic truth as seen by Jude. **Jude 5,** *"I will therefore put you in <u>remembrance</u>, <u>though ye once knew this</u>, how that the Lord, having saved the people out of the land of Egypt, afterward destroyed them <u>that believed not</u>."*

In **Jude 3** Jude tells us he is teaching on the subject of the "common salvation". He then goes on to say, *"Beloved, when I gave all diligence to write unto you of <u>the common salvation</u>, it was needful for me to write unto you, and exhort you that ye should earnestly contend for the faith which was once delivered unto the saints."*

Again, who died in the wilderness? Those who had sinned, those "that believed not." Yet every five-year-old, twelve-year-old, or even nineteen-year-old survived and crossed the Jordan into the Promised Land. They were not **numbered** among those who sinned nor were they **numbered** among those (according to Jude) that *"believed not".*

"How can this even be?" you ask. As we see in Number 14:23, it is because the sins of those under twenty years of age…did not provoke God. **Numbers 14:23,** *"Surely they shall not see the land which I sware unto their fathers, neither shall any of them that provoked me see it."*

Chapter 8

Scripture and Accountability

The writer of Hebrews, under the inspiration of God's Holy Spirit, defines for us in Hebrews 3:17 specifically who died in the wilderness and why. He tells us who God was grieved with and their punishment. The verse makes it clear there were those who, in God's sight, had sinned and in His justice all those who sinned and were accountable for their sins were equally punished. Likewise, all those who did not provoke God were not guilty nor were they accountable in His sight; their carcasses did not fall in the wilderness.

We refer to the "<u>age</u> of grace" as part of our daily Christian conversation but now we must also understand that God gives an age or **period** of grace for every child. This grace is extended to every young person. It is a time that God has set to give all mankind an opportunity to consider good and evil: to **seek** out the difference between good and evil, to genuinely understand good and evil, and, most importantly, to absorb the fact that there are eternal consequences for evil… and that God has made a way to escape the consequences of evil. In our teaching on missions, we emphasize that everyone is "responsible" for their sins whether they have "heard or not heard" and we have volumes of Scripture to support this true doctrine. With confidence we share accounts of natives in the darkest parts of our world, knowing they were not right with their Creator and traveling hundreds of miles to "seek" Truth. Through their effort of finding Truth, God leads them directly to a missionary where they are introduced to Christ and are saved. But, could a seven-year-old do this - a twelve-year-old or a fifteen-year-old? Not likely. God does give mankind twenty years to fill an inner spiritual hunger: to be taught, to become curious, to learn, even to seek, so that God may say in **Romans 1:20,** *"For the invisible things of him from the creation of the world are clearly seen, being understood by the things that are made, even his eternal power and Godhead; so that <u>they are without excuse:</u>".* Could God say, "they are without excuse" if they were five years old, or eleven years old? No, God gives every soul a chance to wonder at the creation around them and seek out Who it is that performed this marvelous act.

But with whom was he grieved forty years? was it not with them that had sinned, whose carcases fell in the wilderness?

– Hebrews 3:17

To not be accountable, one must be in a place free from the penalty for sin. That is how we must understand the matter of King David's son. We understand Scripture to clearly teach **Romans 3:23,** *"For all have sinned, and come short of the glory of God;".* We never question or argue that, but, for David's son to be in Heaven, there must be an explanation. The explanation is that God gives a period of time when man will not be held eternally accountable for their sins, their sin nature or even their unbelief. There is a period of time wherein God is not "provoked" by their sins. How else did David's son end up in Heaven? He was born in iniquity. We know that from **Psalm 51:5** *"Behold, I was shapen in iniquity; and in sin did my mother conceive me."* Whether we choose two years of age or twenty years of age, we must have a doctrine to stand on. How did David's son not go to Hell if he was conceived in sin? It could only be by grace! There can be no other explanation. Grace is the unmerited favor of God. In the case of children, biblically speaking, from conception up to twenty years of age, it is a period of time when God does not hold them eternally accountable for their sins if they die before reaching the age of twenty. An age of innocence - not innocent of sin or sinning, but rather judged innocent by the Great Judge, the King of kings and Lord of lords. All because of grace.

It is only God's grace that makes us to be "without sin". It is only God's grace that allows God, the omniscient One, to be able to say in **Psalm 103:6-17,**

"The LORD executeth righteousness and judgment for all that are oppressed. He made known his ways unto Moses, his acts unto the children of Israel. The LORD is merciful and gracious, <u>slow to anger, and plenteous in mercy</u>. He will not always chide: neither will he keep his anger for ever. He hath not dealt with us after our sins; nor rewarded us according to our iniquities. For as the heaven is high above the earth, so great is his mercy toward them that fear him. As far as the east is from the west, so far hath he removed our transgressions from us. Like <u>as a father pitieth his children</u>, so the LORD pitieth them that fear him. For he knoweth our frame; he remembereth that we are dust. As for man, his days are as grass: as a flower of the field, so he flourisheth. For the wind passeth over it, and it is gone; and the place thereof shall know it no more. But the mercy of the LORD is from everlasting to everlasting upon them that fear him, and his righteousness unto <u>children's children;</u>"

We learn from Paul's writing to the church at Corinth about the wilderness wanderings of the children of Israel: **1 Corinthians 10:11**, *"Now all these things happened unto them for <u>ensamples</u>: and they are written for our admonition, upon whom the ends of the world are come."* As we read of all that happened to the children of Israel we must note how God dealt with each and every one of them. As we focus on this idea of God's grace we cannot help but look at a verse like Psalm 103:17 with fresh eyes: **Psalm 103:17** *"But the mercy of the LORD is from everlasting to everlasting upon them that fear him, <u>and</u> his righteousness unto children's children;"*

I see two groups of people allowed to enter the promised land:

1. Those "men" who **<u>feared</u>** God…Joshua and Caleb
2. **<u>Children's children</u>**…those under the age of twenty and even the children born during the wilderness journeys.

This is why, I believe, while teaching a series on the wilderness wanderings of God's people, the question of the age of accountability came into my mind. **Psalm 103:7**, *"He made known <u>his ways</u> unto Moses, his acts unto the children of Israel."* and all these things that happened were for "…our **admonition**" and as "**ensamples**" for you and I.

The way He dealt with the children of Israel is the way He will deal with you and I today. **Malachi 3:6**, *"For I am the LORD, I change not; therefore ye sons of Jacob are not consumed."* Because God changes not, His promises are for every generation.

Because we compare God's love to ours, God's long-suffering to ours, His love and His long-suffering make no sense to us. In America, it is normal for a person who commits a crime to be tried as an adult at eighteen years of age. But the very next verse explains this as well. **Psalm 103:8,** *"The LORD is merciful and gracious, slow to anger, and plenteous in mercy."* God gives us twenty years to "grow up", twenty years to figure it all out, twenty years before we are asked to face the reality of war or the eternal consequences of sin. God is consistent in all of this because it is His mercy and grace that surpasses our own understanding. **Romans 11:33,** *"O the depth of the riches both of the wisdom and knowledge of God! how unsearchable are his <u>judgments</u>, and his ways past finding out!"*

God created us. He knows our limitations and our tendency to skepticism. Scripture goes on to explain this truth when we read in, **Psalm 103:14,** *"For he knoweth our frame; he remembereth that we are dust".* In the next chapter we will touch on the development of the human body. You will see that the Creator God, indeed, "knoweth our frame". We will see more clearly and more convincingly why God gives us this period of grace to allow us the time to develop our understanding of the need to be saved. Once we grasp the understanding of this wonderful period that God gives each soul, we find ourselves embracing this age of grace as a beautiful picture of God's overall grace towards mankind. Jonah was angry with God because of His longsuffering and forgiveness of the people of Nineveh. Let us now be careful to accept a doctrine that demonstrates those very same attributes of grace and longsuffering.

Looking back at **Hebrews 3:17,** *"But with whom was he grieved forty years? was it not with <u>them that had sinned</u>, <u>whose carcases fell</u> in the wilderness?".* We remind ourselves that there was a specific group of people that God was grieved with. It was those who should have known better; who understood the decision they were making when they told Moses they would rather return to Egypt than go into this new land that God had promised them. It was those old enough to fully understand "good and evil" and understand the consequences of their decisions. Though this land had been promised them by God Himself, they in unbelief, had rejected it. These are the people God would be grieved with and these are the only ones who would die before entering into the promise. Yes... it was only those who were twenty years of age and upward. Those under the age of twenty would be ushered into the promised land without penalty.

One last time we see this same truth in *Numbers 32:13 "And the LORD's anger was kindled against Israel, and he made them wander in the wilderness* *forty years, until all the generation, that had done evil <u>in the sight of the LORD, was consumed</u>".* I hope you find this as eye-opening as I did. God's ways are not our ways. When a teen cried out against Moses and against God...He did not record it as "evil". They were in a different category. They had not yet reached the age of accountability in God's sight.

Chapter 9

The Science

David acknowledged that we are fearfully and wonderfully made. Men and women dedicate their lives, many years of study and preparation, to call themselves a "foot specialist", a "hand specialist" or a "kidney specialist"... the list goes on. Man is constantly learning more and more about the human body. It is remarkable to the thinking of a believer that someone could study the human body and not believe in the God who created it. Those of us who do believe, however, are always built up in our faith when we clearly see the Creator's hand in the wonders of the human body. **Romans 1:20**, *"For the invisible things of him from the creation of the world are clearly seen, being understood by the things that are made, even his eternal power and Godhead; so that they are without excuse:"* The subject of accountability is no exception to this truth. Accountability must then, in some way, be linked to man's understanding of how God created us. The age of innocence and the doctrine of accountability must be in harmony with exactly how He created us, how the brain functions and most importantly, how the brain develops.

The brain, in many ways, is functionally developed by age ten. That said, though it is developed, many of the electrical connections are not fully intact. The part of the brain that lets a person understand **consequences** is what scientists call the frontal lobe. The frontal lobe (or prefrontal cortex) is the last part of the brain to be fully developed and connected. Nerve signals, to work properly, must be well insulated by a substance called myelin. Because the formation of myelin in the brain is not 100% present until the mid twenties, it is not until around twenty years of age that a young person has a well-connected frontal lobe allowing them to process and understand **consequences**. *"...He knoweth our frame..."* **Psalm 103:14** Did God design us to not be fully developmentally capable of understanding consequences until we are twenty, but then make us responsible and eternally accountable for those consequences at age five or seven or even twelve? I submit to you that that possibility cannot exist under anyone's definition of God's grace.

For he knoweth our frame; he remembereth that we are dust.

– Psalm 103:14

Ask a child why he threw a brick through a window and his response, very honestly will be, "I don't know". That is because they really and truly don't know. I remember, as a thirteen-year-old, sitting in my parent's cottage, with my BB-gun aiming at a vintage glass-globed hurricane lamp and pulling the trigger. Guess what happened - yes indeed...the BB hit the globe and shattered it. What in the world was I thinking? I was a deadeye with that BB-gun; I had shot thousands of BB's through it outside, at targets, for years. But, for some reason, completely unknown to me even today, I aimed, pulled the trigger, and shattered that lamp. I was not even able to fully realize the consequences of an action that I clearly understood physically but not morally. I knew exactly what would happen and at the same time did not understand the consequences of pulling that trigger.

Back at that same cottage, four years later (now a "man" at seventeen with a driver's license in my wallet), I was driving my parents' car down a dirt road doing over 100 miles an hour. What is it about a teenager and speed? I didn't know then what it was, but I gave no thought whatsoever to the possible consequences of driving that fast. Looking back, it was only by God's grace that I did not kill someone, or myself, or even get caught in this dangerous act. What I do remember is that the STOP sign came up on me much faster than it would at 45 miles an hour and I flew through it at nearly 100 mph with my brakes fully engaged. Thankfully, no one was out on this normally much-travelled crossroad. The problem though, thinking back on that time, is that at seventeen I somehow did not understand the consequences of such foolish and dangerous behavior. Nor, with a brain still in development, could I fully understand those consequences. I had been taught, trained, and warned about safe driving but drove in this manner anyway.

What I do know is that you don't have to use my childhood example of foolishness to understand this truth. I am sure you have a list of your own experiences that will help convince you of this developmental phenomenon. Can you remember an example in your own life when you were old enough to know something but not old enough to understand it at the time? Do you remember an experience in your life when you were old enough to hold a sword and shield, yet not "able to **handle**" that same sword and shield? Can you think back on freedoms given to you by your parents that you both squandered and abused? Perhaps memories of your first smoke, first drink, first immoral act or first experimental drug come rushing to your mind and you think "Why did I do that?" "What in the world was I thinking?" This is why we often say as adults, "Too soon old and too late smart".

Let me clarify at this point - I would have and should have been held fully responsible to civil authorities had I been caught, or if I had caused a terrible accident. (As I write this book it makes me think perhaps, we ought not be allowed to drive before twenty years of age!) My attempt here is to simply point out our lack of maturity even though the government says we are now old enough to do something. We need to understand there is a creational reason why we lack the ability to fully recognize the consequences of our actions.

The prefrontal cortex or PFC is the explanation for teenagers' lack of maturity. Let me qualify myself here, please - no, let me disqualify myself or unqualify myself here as an authority on the subject of brain development. I am no doctor, nurse, or medical expert of any sort. Thankfully, there are places to go and people to learn from about this matter. It is essential that I cover this subject thoroughly because it was the second thing that made me decide that this book must be written. Let me challenge you. When you have completed this book, go to your favorite search engine and type in any of the following phrases: brain development, the teen brain, frontal lobe development, or frontal lobe functions. You name it and it will amaze you. I have no idea how anyone could spend one hour reading any or all of these articles and not immediately agree that God's special biblical age of twenty is one of His most loving, gracious and merciful truths in Scripture. And it is a very special proof that He is indeed the Creator because **"...he knoweth our frame..." Psalm 103:14** and knew all along that "twenty years of age and upward" was the only reasonable age for making someone eternally accountable for their actions.

Phase two of my curiosity started one day when I was talking with my sister (who knew absolutely nothing of my interest in the age of accountability). My sister mentioned she had been watching a daytime television show and a doctor was being interviewed. In that interview the doctor was discussing teenagers and why they do some of the crazy things they do. We love to blame a teenager's problems on hormones but there seems to be a much more important reason for the way a teenager acts and behaves. We must take into consideration a teen's PFC development. How can a young person who seems to have everything and has loving parents, then suddenly, unexpectedly blow up at them and say, "you never do anything for me! - you don't love me" or worse yet, "I hate you!" In reality, though they say it, they know they don't hate you and you know they don't hate you. How can they not think about what those words will do to their parents? Fortunately, there is actually a real answer. They genuinely do not understand the consequences of what they are saying or doing.

This same science helps us to understand why bullying is so prevalent among our young. A child is bullied, badgered and bruised until they cannot bear to go to school and in worse scenarios, either take their own life or tragically decide to take the life of someone else in retaliation. In the aftermath of such horrific scenes, those who did the bullying cannot understand why such a terrible thing happened. Clearly and genuinely, they do not understand that their bullying also has consequences. This bewilderment is not an act they are putting on. They genuinely don't understand. This truth places a great burden on parents and on all adults to guide our youth, to watch over them, and teach them not to bully and to help our children when they are bullied. We must be their consciences for them until they can think clearly for themselves.

The importance of the role of parents during these first twenty years.

Though a subject for another book, it is mandatory that I take a few minutes and point out the importance of the role of parents. Having established that a young person does not have the ability to grasp long-term consequences fully, what should you and I do as parents? We must step in and perform the role of their pre-frontal cortex. Not only are we responsible for teaching them right from wrong, but we closely monitor them and prevent them from making those terrible choices that will harm them in the long term. This responsibility, as parents, does not end when they are twelve, sixteen, or even eighteen. The parent must take on this responsibility until such a time as their child's reasoning is able to handle this all-important job. We must keep in mind, however, that while a young person is not accountable for their sins regarding eternity, they are fully responsible for their actions to parents and to society, and will answer to civil authorities.

Let's look at just one of the costs of going against God's Word in our society. With my twenty years of military service, I have a great interest in the debilitating effects of PTSD (Post-traumatic stress disorder). Knowing what Scripture says about the God-given age to enter military service I was not surprised to find an article entitled: "Younger Soldiers in Combat Are Seven Times More Likely to Develop PTSD". In this article the author quotes William Tecumseh Sherman, a general during the Civil War, who told the graduating class of the Michigan Military Academy in 1879 that, "There is many a boy here today who looks on war as all glory, but, boys, it is all h---."

Digging deeper I found, with great interest, non-Christian movements attempting to change the legal age to join the US Forces to twenty-one. This movement is based on the science (not the Scripture) that the brain is not developed well enough for a younger person to fully understand what they are getting into and what they are dealing with in war. It is not all glory. They are not bulletproof. Nor is it a video game where they will be given seven lives for each battle and with a push of the "reset" button they can start the game over. Young people do not understand the feelings and emotions they will suffer when they know their bullet, or their bomb took the life of another human being. The trauma of seeing their friends and fellow soldiers killed in their sight, the faces and the memories of war - this will never leave them. War is never easy, and we should not expect someone to enter a situation, like military service, where the Scriptures specifically prohibit them from being involved. No age is immune from the horrors of war but God knows, those under twenty are far more likely to develop PTSD. Sadly, it brings lifelong emotional effects.

For sure, those under twenty years old are physically able to carry a sword and shield. But they are not "able" to do so since they do not understand the consequences of rushing into battle.

This is not a book on science, and I am realistic enough to know that most of my readers are not going to follow any type of a technical explanation of the brain and its development. But the correlation of brain development, creation, Creator, and God's grace is so important that I felt this rudimentary explanation of brain development should be inserted. Again, if you wish to have an even greater confidence in your understanding of the age of accountability, take some time and do some independent studies on the brain's development. The more articles you read the more you will see that the God who formed us is the same God who gives us twenty years to make a spiritual decision for Christ.

Chapter 10

When Sin Is Not Imputed

As it is with any study, seeking one answer raises many new questions. One such question for me was what exactly happens to the sins of someone, prior to the age of accountability who has not trusted Christ as their Savior? This seemed to be a huge problem doctrinally and without an answer to this question I was at a standstill. I was at an impasse because the Bible is clear in **Romans 3:23**, *"For all have sinned, and come short of the glory of God;"* Speaking of Heaven we are told in **Revelation 21:27**, *"And there shall in no wise enter into it any thing that defileth, neither whatsoever worketh abomination, or maketh a lie: but they which are written in the Lamb's book of life."*

I touched on this truth in the preface pointing out there was a time in Paul's life when the Law did not pertain to him. **Romans 7:9**, *"For <u>I was alive without the law once</u>: but when the commandment came, sin revived, and I died."* As an adult, Paul could look back at a time when he was without the Law. How could this possibly be when the Law had been given over 1,500 years prior to the birth of Paul? Paul had been trained up in the Old Testament law from a child, yet he would write about a time when he was without it. Paul was also aware of a time when the Law "came" into his life personally and when it did come into his life "**sin revived**". Sin was made alive in him and at that very point Paul died! He died because he had not trusted Christ during his first twenty years. He understood that he died, at that point, spiritually. He was not dead before that day. Before that time or even before that moment Paul was alive but thereafter, spiritually - he was dead. Sins committed during the age of innocence are not imputed against us at that time. They are, however, recorded and we will be held eternally responsible for them if we do not accept Christ as our personal Savior after reaching the age of eternal accountability. If one dies as David's son did, or as a youth, they are, by the grace of God, not eternally judged for those sins and are granted Heaven as their home.

There are two conditions for entering Heaven. We cannot enter with sin imputed to us and we must have our name written in the Lamb's Book of Life –Rev 21:27. Only those whose names are written in the Lamb's book of life can enter into heaven.

"...sin is not imputed when there is no law."

– Romans 5:13b

We must then agree that at conception God writes our names into the Lamb's Book of Life. Through our first twenty years our name is there. It must be so because we know **Psalm 51:5**, ***"Behold, I was shapen in iniquity; and in sin did my mother conceive me."*** We are not sinners because we sin...we sin because we are sinners. As Paul points out, there was a period when the Law did not pertain to him. This is because his name, at conception, was written in the Lamb's Book of Life. But then, at twenty years of age, with all his religion and works, the commandments were levied against him, sin revived and he, at that moment died and was in need of salvation and in desperate need of being "born again" through Christ.

It would seem, according to Scripture, that everyone's name that has ever been conceived has been recorded in the Book of Life. The very name of the book helps us to understand exactly what this book is all about. It is a book that records every soul ever given "life". Either the first birth or the born-again experience. Thus, we have the title... the Book of Life. Everyone is given a time-sensitive reservation in Heaven at conception. A reservation with an "expiration if not claimed by" date. The name is written, at birth, in pencil. Then, after we trust Christ it is recorded in ink, indelible ink, permanent marker.

In fact, every name was placed in the Book long before we were even born. We learn in Scripture that both the actions of the slain Lamb and His Book of

Life have a copyright dated from the foundation of the world. Those who reach the age of accountability but have not made the all-important decision to trust Jesus Christ as their personal Savior then have their name removed and they are without hope of Heaven. **Revelation 13:8,** *"And all that dwell upon the earth shall worship him, whose names are not written in the book of life of the Lamb slain <u>from the foundation of the world</u>. And Revelation 17:8 The beast that thou sawest was, and is not; and shall ascend out of the bottomless pit, and go into perdition: and they that dwell on the earth shall wonder, whose names were not written in the book of life <u>from the foundation of the world</u>, when they behold the beast that was, and is not, and yet is."*

We enter into a deep doctrinal area without the time here to fully deal with it. Looking at a timeline of our life, we might see we are conceived when our name, from the foundation of the world, is already written in the Lamb's Book of Life. For our first twenty years, our name rests safely there. When we turn twenty our name is removed if we have not, during our twenty years of opportunity, trusted as our Savior. If at some point after turning twenty, we come to our spiritual senses and accept Christ, then our name is placed back into the Book that has existed since the foundation of the world. And, this is still the same book, where our name had originally been written since the foundation of the world.

Revelation 3:5 has long been a stumbling block for those of us who strongly believe that we cannot lose our salvation. Up to this point we have given somewhat weak explanations about what this "overcometh" could actually mean. **Revelation 3:5,** *"He that overcometh, the same shall be clothed in white raiment; and <u>I will not blot out his name out of the book of life</u>, but I will confess his name before my Father, and before his angels."* As we consider this verse in relationship to our subject we can certainly apply the action of a name being blotted out of the Book of Life to our leaving the age of innocence and entering the age of accountability. This is the one and only time our name can be blotted out. By accepting Christ in our youth, we make good use of the time God has given us and the expiration date on our name is removed in the Book of Life and our name is now written in permanent ink.

Like Paul, prior to you and I being accountable to God for the Law, spiritually speaking, we were alive. We were still responsible for social laws and even religious laws before man, but not eternally before God. Then, at twenty years of age, if we have not received and accepted the Gospel and Jesus Christ as our Savior, the

commandment to obey the Law, along with the consequences for disobedience is put into effect. Now sin and the penalty for sin, past, present and future, is made alive in us and we "die" without Christ. And...our name is removed from the Book.

Paul was a Jew and an enemy of the church and an enemy of God. When accountability to the Law came to Paul...he died. When Paul is writing to Timothy we find quite a different story in the life of Timothy. **2 Timothy 1:5**, *"When I call to remembrance the <u>unfeigned faith</u> that is in thee, which dwelt first in thy grandmother Lois, and thy mother Eunice; and I am persuaded that in thee also."* We are not told exactly when Timothy accepted Christ, but we read that his faith was unfeigned. Unfeigned meaning it was not counterfeit nor was it hypocritical. It was real and sincere. How often do we see a child raised in church act "good", but once they are out from under their parents' roof, they demonstrate their true nature (a sin nature)? It does not have to be this way, but so often it is. Not so with Timothy. From his grandmother, to his mother and now to Timothy - true faith. If a person places their faith in Christ before the Law is levied against them, their names are not removed from the Lamb's Book of Life when they reach the age of accountability. Timothy, it would seem, never lived a day outside God's grace. This is the love of God and this is God's plan. We are born, and given many years to learn, to grow and to trust Christ.

In Jesus' teaching we learn exactly what the kingdom of God consists of. **Luke 18:16-17** *"But Jesus called them unto him, and said, Suffer little children to come unto me, and forbid them not: <u>for of such is the kingdom of God</u>. Verily I say unto you, Whosoever shall not receive the kingdom of God as a little child shall in no wise enter therein."* The kingdom of God is filled with children. Imagine for a moment all the souls of the children from Africa, China, India, Pakistan, Iran, Iraq and all around the world since creation who are in Heaven today. "Red and yellow, black and white, they are precious in His sight, Jesus loves the little children of the world." All of them, from conception to twenty years of age: He claims them.

Except we come to Him like a little child we will never know Heaven as our home. And how does a child come? Interestingly, they come from a position of grace. They come from a place not of fear, but of feeling the love of God unconditionally. We don't come to God just for a Get Out of Hell pass, to go to Heaven. Rather, we come to Him because of all that He has done for us and most importantly we are to love Him...because He first loved us. We are to come to Him because He is...God.

When Sin Is Not Imputed 63

Societal laws are based on these same truths of the need for young people to understand consequences. A juvenile breaks a law. He is placed, not in the normal legal system, but rather, into the juvenile system. The very terminology that is used is a great example of how God deals with His children. A child is placed into the juvenile system rather than the criminal justice system. Wow! To begin with, the very names of these systems are interesting. An underaged law breaker is called a "juvenile delinquent" while an adult law breaker is called a "criminal". The difference between the juvenile system and the adult system is that the juvenile system focuses much more on teaching and rehabilitation, while the adult system focuses on punishment. Why? Because society feels adults are accountable for their actions, while juveniles are not accountable because they truly did not understand the consequences of what they were doing. Yes, they should have known better…but they did not fully understand the consequences.

Our legal system has another illustration of what happens to a young person in relationship to their sins. A young person's crimes are expunged. In the legal system the word **expunged** means **erase or remove completely (something unwanted or unpleasant)**. Though the definition would tell us those crimes were erased or removed, the reality is that they can be opened by certain authorities in the case of a security clearance or when requesting a visa for another country. Likewise, prior to twenty years of age, we sin but are not eternally accountable for those sins at that time. We have to understand that God keeps a record of all our transgressions: all of our sins, all of our works. We know this from **Revelation 20:12,** *"And I saw the dead, small and great, stand before God; and the books were opened: and another book was opened, which is the book of life: and the dead were judged out of those things which were written in the books, according to their works."*

So there is a period during which when we sin, God knows that we have sinned, He records those sins in His books, yet a young person will not be held eternally accountable for those sins if they should die before they turn twenty years old. How can that possibly be? Paul explains this truth to us, as one who lived a period of his life without the commandments, rejecting Christ. Then, when he became accountable, he "died" spiritually because of those same sins. He tells us the answer in **Romans 5:13,** *"For until the law sin was in the world: but sin is not <u>imputed</u> when there is no law."*

Imputed – (Webster def) "Charged to the account of; attributed; ascribed. Yes, there was transgression and yes, it is even recorded, but it is not imputed against one who has not reached the age of accountability. When they reach that age, sin is then imputed and they "die".

This gives us a deeper understanding of **Galatians 3:24-25,** *"Wherefore the law was our schoolmaster to bring us unto Christ, that we might be justified by faith. But after that faith is come, we are no longer under a schoolmaster."* Like the juvenile system, there are laws, and when we break those laws there are lesser punishments for those still in the age of innocence so that they might learn from those laws. Paul explains this as "not being under the Law". Those laws are a schoolmaster to us. But because you have broken those laws and because you are a born sinner, as an adult you will pay eternally for those same sins if you are without Christ. We are given those twenty years to allow the laws that exist to draw us to Christ. Like the example of diplomatic immunity - we are expected to obey the laws, yet, at the same time, we are exempt from the penalty of those very laws. Then, when we come to Christ, we no longer need that schoolmaster. **Romans 6:14,** *"For sin shall not have dominion over you: for ye are not under the law, but under grace."* And, when we reach that age of accountability, if we have accepted Christ, we are not "accountable" and no sin will ever be imputed against us. All of our sins are much more than "expunged"... for us, they are as far as the east is from the west and in God's sight they are remembered no more. (Ps. 103:12)

Chapter 11

From Twenty Years Old and Upward

There is a question that kept coming up in my own mind, so I know as a reader that same question may be in your mind as well. "You mean, exactly on a person's twentieth birthday this all happens?" Having, myself, struggled with this in the past, I have accepted that the answer to this question is, YES.

In Old Testament times, if I were a father and they were trying to draft my son to go to war I might very well say, "His birthday is not till next month and he is not eligible according to God's Word, to go into battle". If the temple tax collector were to come to my home and when my wife and I, with six children, had been told I had to "pay tax" for them I would very likely have said, "None of them have reached their twentieth birthday just yet so you cannot, scripturally, collect that tax!"

Today, if a military recruiter were to come to my home and say that my son or daughter wanted to join the military and they were seventeen, I would point out that my child cannot make that decision, without my consent, until they have reached their eighteenth birthday - not one day before. And there is nothing the recruiter or the young person could do to change that.

I am constrained then to simply apply the same reasoning to "the age of accountability". Otherwise, there is still a period of time when one may not "know" where they stand with God. Everyone has the right to know that they are either lost or saved according to God's Word.

This is a tool we might use in our teaching and preaching to teens in the future.

From twenty years old and upward, all that are able to go forth to war in Israel: thou and Aaron shall number them by their armies.

— Numbers 1:3

Chapter 12

A Later Age Fits with the Attributes of God

When we look at the age of TWENTY as the age where one becomes eternally accountable to God for their sins, we see one last truth. This age fits every attribute we relate to our God. Taking the most common and best known or agreed on attributes of God note how this age is a perfect example of our eternal, loving, immutable and longsuffering God.

1. Infinite – Past, present and future. Because of this Peter tells us, **2 Peter 3:8**, *"But, beloved, be not ignorant of this one thing, that one day is with the Lord as a thousand years, and a thousand years as one day."* When the One who is eternal looks at a day or a thousand years, they are insignificant periods of time. When we, who are given seventy years, look at twenty years it is almost a third of our lifetime and seems too "generous". To God it is exactly the correct amount of time to allow someone to make an eternal decision.

2. Immutable – He never changes. **Malachi 3:6**, *"For I am the LORD, I change not; therefore ye sons of Jacob are not consumed."* The time God gives us to make such an important decision has never changed. As in the wilderness, it was just as significant when only those twenty and over had to give an offering for atonement or a ransom for their sins. This age of innocence is a gift from God to us.

James 1:17, "Every good gift and every perfect gift is from above, and cometh down from the Father of lights, with whom is no variableness, neither shadow of turning."

3. Omnipotent – All Powerful. Only God and God alone can have this attribute. With man we know from experience, "Power corrupts, and absolute power corrupts absolutely." But with God, His omnipotence allows Him to not only judge perfectly, but to show mercy perfectly. God can look at our rebellion, foolishness, and sins, for twenty years and not be provoked by them.

4. Omniscient – All-knowing. Genesis 2:7, *"And the LORD God formed man of the dust of the ground, and breathed into his nostrils the breath of life; and man became a living soul."* He knows all about us, how we grow and mature. Only He could know and say that twenty years is the perfect amount of time for man's brain to form and mature and to be justly held accountable.

For I am the LORD, I change not; therefore ye sons of Jacob are not consumed.

– Malachi 3:6

5. Faithful – Deuteronomy 7:9, *"Know therefore that the LORD thy God, he is God, the faithful God, which keepeth covenant and mercy with them that love him and keep his commandments to a thousand generations;"* The covenants God made with man thousands of years ago still hold faithfully true today.

6. Good – In all matters but, perhaps specifically, in the matter of this older age of accountability, we might think of His goodness as found in *Isaiah 55:8-9, "For my thoughts are not your thoughts, neither are your ways my ways, saith the LORD. For as the heavens are higher than the earth, so are my ways higher than your ways, and my thoughts than your thoughts.* And then consider Proverbs 25:2 *"It is the glory of God to conceal a thing: but the honour of kings is to search out a matter."* Because every pastor I asked had no real understanding of this subject I felt it best to "search out a matter".

7. Just – Everything God does is perfect. It is always interesting to me to find that the lost world will often say to a believer, "How can a loving and just God send someone to Hell". But then we have no answer whatsoever as to how this same just God deals with the most important thing in our lives: our children and the children around us. Because He is just He will not condemn a child. A child by His definition, not by ours. His ways are just! **Deuteronomy 32:4**, *"He is the Rock, his work is perfect: for all his ways are judgment: a God of truth and without iniquity, just and right is he."*

8. Merciful – We are all thankful for his mercy. When it comes to whom He will show mercy, or at what age He chooses to show his grace and mercy, we might read **Romans 9:15-16**, *"For he saith to Moses, I will have mercy on whom I will have mercy, and I will have compassion on whom I will have compassion. So then it is not of him that willeth, nor of him that runneth, but of God that sheweth mercy."* Clearly, God will do the right and merciful thing always.

9. Gracious – Psalm 145:8, *"The LORD is gracious, and full of compassion; slow to anger, and of great mercy."* When we speak of an eternal God who is gracious and full of compassion, does twenty years really seem so long? I think not. In fact, many parents have waited much longer than twenty years for a wayward child to return.

10. Longsuffering – Perhaps in His longsuffering we see this truth the clearest. We all have our opinions, thoughts and ideas. We have seen our ways are not His ways. And we are thankful His ways are different. Though we love our children we can get irritated with them, we can give up on them, we can even turn from them. But God cannot. He is the definition of longsuffering. He is longsuffering. Once again the down to earth, rubber-meets-the-road guy, Peter, is used to help us understand this when he writes, **"2 Peter 3:9,** *"The Lord is not slack concerning his promise, as some men count slackness; but is longsuffering to us-ward, not willing that any should perish, but that all should come to repentance."*

Chapter 13

How Does This Affect My Life and My Ministry?

nce you have this doctrinal truth settled in your mind so many things will change in your view of Christianity, and even of God. His attributes become clearer. God becomes what we have always known Him to be, a loving God. Now we see a side of Him that for some reason we never before cared about, or even considered.

If there is one thing most Bible-believing Christians agree on, it would be our stand against abortion. If you could now take your understanding of God's grace toward the unborn and extend that grace through to their twentieth birthday, it would help you in so many ways. You could then understand the difficult "tween" years, you could patiently work through their rebellious and often sinful teen years and realize that, given the time God has allotted them - twenty years - they will actually, physically, emotionally and spiritually come to their senses.

As parents, if our children do not get saved during devotions at five or seven years of age, we will no longer feel that we have failed. This new understanding makes **I Cor 3:7** all the more important to us. *"So then neither is he that planteth any thing, neither he that watereth; but God that giveth the increase."*

Parents will no longer need to feel like their seven-year-old is standing on the very precipice of Hell. Ministry workers can patiently and lovingly use Scripture to build a foundation of understanding for their young people. In essence, we can all relax and enjoy children - once we embrace the biblical understanding of twenty years, instead of an unknown age.

In **Isaiah 28:9-13** we read:

"Whom shall he teach knowledge? and whom shall he make to understand doctrine? them that are weaned from the milk, and drawn from the breasts. For precept must be upon precept, precept upon precept; line upon line, line upon line; here a little, and there a little: For with stammering lips and another tongue will he speak to this people. To whom he said, This is the rest wherewith ye may cause the weary to rest; and this is the refreshing: yet they would not hear. But the word of the LORD was unto them precept upon precept, precept upon precept; line upon line, line upon line; here a little, and there a little; that they might go, and fall backward, and be broken, and snared, and taken."

These things have I written unto you that believe on the name of the Son of God; that ye may know that ye have eternal life, and that ye may believe on the name of the Son of God.

– 1 John 5:13

Though the context of this passage has been understood in a number of different ways, one truth is undeniable. God is not pleased with those "men" who feel God's way of teaching is not for them. Hearing, learning and understanding the ways of God is designed to be taught slowly and carefully. *"...precept upon precept, precept upon precept; line upon line, line upon line, here a little, and there a little..."* **Isa 28:10**

When sharing Christ with others; whether door to door, family members, co-workers or cashiers, it is important that we understand each person's standing before God as we speak with them. Young and old. John teaches us in **1 John 5:13,** *"These things have I written unto you that believe on the name of the Son of God; that ye may know that ye have eternal life, and that ye may believe on*

the name of the Son of God." Now, hopefully, you do know that no matter the age of the person you are witnessing to, you know how God views their sins.

Let's say, for example, you feel God has opened a door for you to speak of salvation to someone, anyone. You gather up your nerve and ask the question that has been asked so many times. Just a way to get into a spiritual conversation, you say, "If you were to die today, do you know for certain where you would spend eternity?" This is a wonderful way to get someone thinking. Now, what if they turned the question around and asked, "If I were to die today, do you know where I would spend eternity?"- a forty-year-old man, yes, you know. A thirty-year-old woman -yes, you know. But, Childrens' Church worker, what about a ten-year-old? Teen class worker, what about twelve, or fifteen?

Understanding the age of accountability will help missionaries realize they have twenty years to bring young people into their homes, teach them, influence them and get to know them, watch as they develop into young adults. As these young people make mistakes, the missionary can better understand why and help them work through the difficult years in order to raise up a new generation of born-again believers.

We should always teach with passion, but we do not need to teach children with panic and fear, either in our own hearts or placed into theirs.

There could be revival worldwide if we simply allow God to work in the hearts of one new generation while we simply, slowly and carefully teach His Word and watch as He gives the increase.

Appendix I
All Scripture References Used

Old Testament

Genesis 2:7 – pg. 68

Exodus 12:51 – pg. 40
23:7 – pg. 8
30:12 – pg. 24
130:4-15 – pg. 20, 21, 22, 23, 24
32:35 – pg. 41

Numbers 1:3 – pg. 27, 28, 66
13:33 – pg. 41
14:1-4 – pg. 42
14:9-10 – pg. 42
14:22-23 – pg. 42, 45
14:26-33 – pg. 43, 44
32:13 – pg. 50, 51

Deuteronomy 1:37-39 – pg. 40, 44
7:9 – pg. 68
32:4 – pg. 69

Judges 8:20 – pg. 31

I Samuel 1:11 – pg. 36
1:22, 24 – pg. 36
1:25 – pg. 36
1:27 – pg. 36
2:11 – pg. 36
2:18 – pg. 36
2:21 – pg. 36
2:26 – pg. 36
3:1 – pg. 35, 36

I Samuel 3:8 – pg. 36, 37
3:19-20 – pg. 37
4:1 – pg. 37
17:26 – pg. 42

II Samuel 12:1-24 – pg. 1, 2, 12, 13, 14

I Chronicles 23:24-32 – pg. 34, 35

II Chronicles 25:2-5 – pg. 29, 30

Ezra 3:8 – pg. 34

Psalm 51:5 – pg. 8, 48, 49, 60
95:10-11 – pg. 7
103:6-17 – pg. 48, 49, 50, 54, 55, 64
106:38 - pg. 8
145:8 - pg. 69

Proverbs 25:2 - pg. 68

Isaiah 7:16 - pg. 44
28:9-13 - pg. 72
40:1 - pg. 12
55:8-9 - pg. 68

Malachi 3:6 – pg. 49, 67, 68

Appendix II
All Scripture References Used

New Testament

Matt 18:3-4 – pg. 7, 8

Mark 10:14-15 – pg. 7

Luke 18:16-17 – pg. 62

John 3:3 – pg. 6
3:7 – pg. 6
9:23 – pg. 22

Acts 22:3 – pg. 5

Romans 1:20 – pg. 48, 53
3:23 – pg. xi, 8, 48, 59
5:13 – pg. 60, 63
6:14 – pg. 64
6:23 – pg. xi
7:7-9, – pg. 36
8: – pg. 36,
9:15-16 – pg. 36
11:33 – pg. 36

I Corinthians 3:7 – pg. 71
10:11 – pg. 49

II Corinthians 1:3-4 – pg. 14

Galatians 3:24-25 – pg. 64

I Thessalonians 4:18 – pg. 2
5:11 – pg. 2

I Timothy 4:12 – pg. 22

II Timothy 1:15 – pg. 62
3:16 – pg. 16

Hebrews 3:17 – pg. 47, 48, 50

James 1:17 – pg. 68

II Peter 3:8-9 – pg. 67, 69

I John 5:11-13 – pg. 3, 4, 17, 72, 73

Jude 3 – pg. 45
5 – pg. 45

Revelation 13:8 – pg. 61
17:8 – pg. 61
20:12 – pg. 63
21:27 – pg. 59, 60

Appendix 1

Appendix III
Additional Old Testament Verses to Consider
(Not Referenced In This Book)

New Testament

Exodus 38:26, 32:32, 33

Proverbs 22:6

Ecclesiastes 11:9, 10

Psalms 58:3

Isaiah 28:9, 10

II Corinthians 15:13

Ezekiel 16:21

Leviticus 27:2-7

About the Author

Jerry Boritzki holds both a bachelors and masters degree in religious education, and is a winner of a National Freedom Foundation at Valley Forge award in writing for published works. He retired from the U. S. Navy in 1990 with twenty years active duty service and is now retired from full-time ministry since 2020. He has been happily married for 52 years, a father of six and grandfather of sixteen. For over twenty years the subject of this book has weighed on his heart and mind. After searching for books on the subject and asking pastors and religious educators their thoughts on this doctrine, it became abundantly clear that a book on this all-important, yet completely neglected truth had to be written.

Contact

JerryBoritzki@ageofaccountability.com
ageofaccountability.com

www.ingramcontent.com/pod-product-compliance
Lightning Source LLC
Chambersburg PA
CBHW060848050426
42453CB00008B/894